OLD-TIME NEW ENGLAND COOKBOOK

Duncan MacDonald
and
Robb Sagendorph

with Decorations by Scott Maclain

DOVER PUBLICATIONS, INC.
NEW YORK

This Dover edition, originally published in 1993, is an
unabridged republication of *Rain, Hail, ... and Baked Beans:
A New England Seasonal Cook Book*, published by Ives Washburn,
Inc., New York, in 1958.

Library of Congress Cataloging-in-Publication Data

MacDonald, Duncan, Broadcaster.
   [Rain, hail, and baked beans]
   Old-time New England cookbook / Duncan MacDonald
and Robb Sagendorph ; with decorations by Scott Maclain.
      p.   cm.
   "An unabridged republication of Rain, hail, and baked
beans . . . published by Ives Washburn, Inc., New York, in
1958"—T.p. verso.
   Includes index.
   ISBN-13: 978-0-486-27630-4
   ISBN-10: 0-486-27630-9
   1. Cookery, American—New England style. I. Sagendorph,
Robb Hansell. II. Title.
TX715.2.N48M33 1993
641.5974—dc20   92-47279
                                             CIP

Manufactured in the United States by Courier Corporation
27630910   2015
www.doverpublications.com

Contents

		PAGE
FOREWORDS		vii
THE NINE SEASONS		
1. EARLY FALL (SEPTEMBER 10–OCTOBER 20)		3
2. FALL (OCTOBER 21–DECEMBER 1)		33
3. EARLY WINTER (DECEMBER 2–JANUARY 10)		51
4. WINTER (JANUARY 11–FEBRUARY 20)		66
5. EARLY SPRING (FEBRUARY 21–APRIL 1)		88
6. SPRING (APRIL 2–MAY 10)		105
7. EARLY SUMMER (MAY 11–JUNE 20)		120
8. SUMMER (JUNE 21–AUGUST 1)		140
9. END OF SUMMER (AUGUST 2–SEPTEMBER 9)		165
FAVORITE RECIPES FROM NEW ENGLAND INNS		185
INDEX		210

THAT this is called a "seasonal cookbook" means that it is designed to serve you just as your calendar does, giving you current information as day by day you turn over the pages. The recipes call for vegetables, fruits, meat, and fish on the market at the time, and result in dishes suitable to the seasonal temperatures.

Up to this time the obstance to writing such a book was that weather just didn't seem to pay much attention to the calendar. In New England, at least, your calendar may say that it's spring, while you are shoveling your driveway clear of snow.

One New England weather prophet, however, is credited with unusual success in spite of his using very unorthodox methods. He is Robb Sagendorph, whose *Old Farmer's Almanac* enrages orthodox weather forecasters with its whimsical explanations of its methods: "Abraham Weatherwise lived in a shack on a dump. He claimed to have a secret weather formula which he had learned through observing the stars between the cracks of the boards in the roof of his shack. His secret formula is the one the present editors use today."

The *Almanac* enrages the orthodox even more when its year-in-advance predictions prove superior to those they've made only a day or two in advance.

With such a weather prophet in collaboration, perhaps a seasonal cookbook will hold up in the face of the treachery of the seasons!

In addition to the notion of weather-appropriate dishes made up of seasonal foods, I like to think that this book will give impetus to the home growing of fruits and vegetables, because I believe that cooks all over the world achieve their greatest successes when they use native products. I hope that among their successes will be some of these dishes derived from the great tradition of Yankee cooking.

DUNCAN MACDONALD

Duncan MacDonald, who writes about food for this book, is known throughout New England for her "Yankee Home and Food Show," broadcast daily over the Yankee Network. She also writes the monthly feature "At Home in New England" for Yankee *magazine.*

A HAPPY home, we say, is that one which finds upon its table just the dish to suit the day!

But how about these New England seasons? Can we say there are only four—spring, summer, winter, and fall? The astronomers do, and they tell us that on or about the twenty-first of June, September, December, and March each of these seasons begins. But any New Englander knows it may or may not be spring on March 21.

The Mayans (3500 B.C.) came nearer to the seasonal truth when they proclaimed a calendar of eighteen twenty-day months. About five thousand years later, after the French Revolution, the French Republic actually proclaimed a forty-day calendar, nine months to the year, which would fit the seasons. And if you stop to think a moment, tradition and legend have always pretty well upheld this forty-day division. Lent is for forty days—so was the Great Deluge—and so, too, is that ever-recurring St. Swithin's Day (July 15) warning of,

"If it rain this day, forty more will follow." Actually, if you wish to pocket New England's weather extremes, the records will fill a forty-day size better and more evenly than any other.

No one has yet invented a safe rule for accurately predicting New England weather, nor is there any confining this weather to the bounds of these forty-day periods. For these reasons, I cannot guarantee it won't be snowing in July on that day when you have prepared a really wonderful hot-weather picnic—or that the birds and bees and flowers won't be on hand for your January skating party. But in the long run these seasons will roll around pretty much as they are outlined here, and you'll be enjoying your meals timed by the clockwork of the stars.

ROBB SAGENDORPH

Robb Sagendorph, editor of The Old Farmer's Almanac *and of* Yankee *magazine, writes of New England weather out of his own knowledge and experience, as well as that of old Abe Weatherwise, the* Almanac's *famous forecaster.*

OLD-TIME
NEW ENGLAND
COOKBOOK

Chapter I   EARLY FALL

September 10–October 20

GONE is summer's sweltering heat. Labor Day is like a signal for the start of autumn schooling, for lawn mowers to vanish, and for rakes and wheelbarrows to appear. The scent of wood-burning fires drifts on the air, and the step of life seems somehow more brisk and snappy. We may relax a few days in the bright warm sun of St. Luke's Little Summer (October 18–21) or during spells of Indian Summer.

Strange idea this Indian Summer. The American Indian, from whom it must have gained its name, undoubtedly knew it as we do—a sudden, surprising, warm spell in September, October, or even November. Traditionally, it almost falls into winter, running from about November 13 on for some two weeks. More often that period is riddled with such happenings as the freeze-over of lakes and rivers, good sleighing in northern states, and the likelihood that at least some snow will be around in almost any year toward the latter part of the month.

On the other hand, New England's finest weather, unexcelled anywhere in the world, is to be enjoyed during October's first three weeks. As a rule, nineteen of these twenty-one days will be cool at night, warm during the day, and colored, of course, with the reds of the turned maples, the yellows of the birch and beech, with an intermixture of all sorts of different hues from other kinds of trees. This is when Indian Summer should be—not the later November date, or any earlier one when the mists of summer may yet be upon us. But who is to argue with tradition? Let us take, regardless of what the calendar says, our fall as it comes. Life is hard by the yard, someone has said, but it's a cinch by the inch.

What could be easier to take than a fall foliage tour into the countryside at this time of year? Or, for that matter, several of them? With the foliage's beauty gradually reaching its height from about September 20 on, by varying one's trips in altitude as well as direction, one may very well catch many different stages of it in one trip—and with several trips, the last one over Columbus Day, you are bound to have caught the peak of autumn coloring.

In places other than New England where foliage colors are not so brilliant or extreme, about September 24 is what is known as Harvest Home Day or, as they call it in Scotland, the "Kirn" or "Mell Supper." Such a day is announced by each farmer when he is satisfied his own particular harvest is in. It is then he passes the word around among his neighbors to come and join him in his feast. With us, no invitation is really necessary. For roadside stands quickly announce when our farmers are ready.

As a novelty some may wish to diversify early fall trips by including one to the coast of Maine, as well as one to Cape Cod. In the case of the former, the contrast of colored maples against the sea will be one you will not forget in a hurry. Pick up some of that native seaweed called dulse while you are about it. Saints of old, you know, lived for years on just this dulse, bread, and water. We have chewed faithfully on the weed from time to time, and must confess that neither its nutritional value nor even its holier aspects held any attraction.

During the Cape Cod trip there will be the marvelous fall coloring of the cranberry bogs to look forward to—as well as the cranberries themselves. These will be in harvest around October 1.

On the way there, however, someone is sure to bring up the subject of hurricanes. And true it is that Nature, getting ready for fall, mixes some mighty curious brews. Gathering up, as she does, summer's excess heat and transferring it overhead to the tropics in ways we don't entirely understand, she sets up a backlash from the tropics of the wind, rain, and warmth we have come to call the hurricane. Perhaps this is because the tropics can't digest all this heat and mugginess of which we have been relieved. We don't know—and nobody else does either. Yet the phenomenon is unforgettable.

5

There is that day or two of yellow lull. Nothing stirs, not even a leaf. The dog's asleep, so is the hired man, and so are all the children and the birds—everything.

Meanwhile, a seemingly calm sea is charging the whole coast line with the thunder of crashing breakers—a dire warning of the roar and destruction of wind and waves to come.

The experts tell us we've had enough hurricanes here in the past decade or two to last us for another hundred years. Except for nostalgic purposes, we may as well forget them and get on with our enjoyment of the Cape and its colors on the bogs.

The full moon nearest the fall equinox (usually September 21) is the Harvest Moon. No other moon stays with us for so long to brighten evening and night in field and forest, nor does any other moon seem as large as this one when it is first full over the horizon.

No one is so unromantic that he or she will not thrill to an outdoor afterdinner excursion of some kind under this moon—in the pine grove, along the beach, up a mountain path, along a lake or river shore.

As September moves into October, we must bid farewell to jacketless and sweaterless days and evenings. The first frosts have come. Darling St. Francis, lover of animals and birds as well as the poor, will be kicking up one of his famous line storms around the fourth of October. Just why these line storms are considered the lashes of St. Francis, tradition does not tell us. Perhaps the good saint is angered, as many are, at the coming of cold weather. Even the term "line storm" itself is not usually understood in many places. Old salts will tell you it means a storm that follows the direction or path of a latitude marker, like the fortieth parallel, into the shore from the sea. However, there is no mistaking it when it does come, and most boat-owners have learned to bring their boats ashore long before its appearance. Many a youthful sailor who has kept his boat out for long enough to test its mettle in this sea and wind has learned how the wind seems heavier in a boat at this time of year, and the waves dull monsters which will not give way to any prow. Seagulls and shore birds will flee before it to inland marshes or ponds. When it is over, the wind will have swung, counterclockwise, around into the cold northwest. It has always been remarked that a northwest wind is "never long in debt" to one from any other point of the compass.

Ever watch these early fall frosts along the bank of a pond or where new soil has been tamped down in a lawn? From what was a flat plain, the freezing of this topsoil makes thousands of tiny islands of ice. Here and there tiny crevasses shoot down into the warmer earth below. So indeed it must be with us any time after the middle of September—the tiny pores of our bodies separated and detached by the change in temperature into an exaggerated topographical map of gooseflesh. Unlike the soil, we tingle with the effects —our blood becomes enlivened in our veins, rushes about even as the animals do on the early morning lawns. We seem opened up, more aware of life.

These weeks are ones in which the surface of the ground is giving off heat as well as dampness. One notices this in mists along the road at dawn as well as dusk. It is easy to

7

imagine all sorts of ghosts and headless horsemen spiraling
up into the day or night from mill ponds as well as lakes.

Now some of the most fascinating of permanent table
centerpieces are to be gathered. Grasses, goldenrod, ferns,
milkweed pods, thistles—the list is endless—have turned a
silvery gray, as if painted by these fall mists. The forms and
parts are all there with only the reds and yellows and blues
gone from them. Some country people will color these stalks
and tendrils by dipping them in a dye or paint to match
the colors in their houses. Others will not venture to pluck
them from their native habitat but take the handsome wide
landscape of nature in this state as the only painting for
their mind's eye.

And so, too, we think we prefer to see this autumn coming
handsomely to its gray and silvery end. How many cocoons
have been left in it—how many of its summer guests have
by now flown south—is anybody's guess. Perhaps the blue-
jays, chickadees, grackles, and other winter birds have come
back to enjoy its store of seeds.

Most of all, there is practically nothing in the landscape
now that will detract from the graceful outline of the
majestic elms and oaks and beeches and maples. There they
stand, as pure in form as Venus herself, and, in their way,
fully as beautiful—testaments to beauty. Our flowers have
gone, our colors, our birds—and we have cleaned the ground
of everything that will keep us during the fall and winter.

Steadfastly one day we notice in the north that all has
become dark and threatening. It will only be wind, we
confidently tell ourselves, a gustiness for a little while—and

then all will be warm and blue and sunny again. It is only when the dark cloud becomes even thicker and the first real ground cover of snow is spewed from it that we turn to these, our friends the trees, to know the solid companionship they will mean to us in the months ahead. The wild rhythm of the dance of their branches against the sullen fall sky is indeed the pattern of life itself—even as the tiny buds, if you examine some of them closely, are already spearheading for spring.

* * *

Food, as we know, has its own eternal relationship with the seasons and their many weathers. These determine when plants will be ripe enough for harvesting, and they also determine whether we should eat more or less of this kind of food or that, in direct relation to the season's temperatures and the activities that it permits or requires.

As the days of September grow cooler, and those of October become crisp, our farms and gardens yield vegetables that call for a hearty serving companion such as a steak, a roast, or a chicken. Cranberries, squash, and pumpkin— their shades of gold and crimson derive from the same brilliant palette of Nature as those of the autumn foliage. So it is that the thrill of swinging around a curve in the road into a burst of leafy color can alternate with the sighting of a roadside stand laden down with its share of the Yankee harvest.

You'll come home, at last, with vegetables only hours away from the fields where they were grown—and with appetites sharpened by the seasonal coolness. Unloading the car, you'll suddenly wonder what led you to buy so much and how in the world you'll be able to use everything before it spoils. The answer to the first question is that the produce looked so beautiful and delicious, nobody could be expected to resist. To the second question there are many mouth-watering answers.

Cranberry Shortcake

2 cups sifted flour	3 tablespoons shortening
4 teaspoons baking powder	¾ cup milk
½ teaspoon salt	2 tablespoons melted butter
	cranberry sauce

Sift dry ingredients, work in shortening, and add milk. Roll out, cut to make two layers for 8-inch pan. Place one layer in pan, spread with melted butter, cover with second layer. Bake in hot oven (425°) about 20 minutes. Place cranberry sauce between layers and on top. Serve hot with whipped cream. Serves 4.

Cranberry Roly-Poly

2 cups sifted flour	⅔ cup milk
3 teaspoons baking powder	2 tablespoons melted butter
½ teaspoon salt	2 cups cranberry sauce
4 tablespoons shortening	drained of juice

Sift dry ingredients together and cut in shortening. Add milk and stir until mixture forms a soft dough. Roll out on lightly floured board to ¼-inch thickness. Brush with melted butter and cover with cranberries. Roll up like jelly roll. Place seam side down on buttered pan and bake in hot oven (425°) 25 to 30 minutes. Serve with hard sauce. Serves 4.

Cranberry Snowballs

1 quart vanilla ice cream	2 cups whole cranberry sauce

shredded coconut

Roll balls of vanilla ice cream in shredded coconut. Spoon cranberry sauce over each snowball and serve. Serves 6.

Cranberry Pie

1 pound cranberries	¼ teaspoon salt
1½ cups sugar	3 tablespoons water
2 tablespoons flour	1 tablespoon melted butter

1 8-inch shell and pie crust

Chop cranberries and mix with remaining ingredients. Fill pie plate lined with pastry, and arrange strips of pie crust crisscross over the top. Bake in a moderate oven (350°) for 45 to 50 minutes.

Cranberry Meringue Pie

1¾ cups sugar	¼ teaspoon salt
¾ cup water	2 tablespoons butter
1 pound cranberries	1 teaspoon vanilla
4 eggs, separated	4 tablespoons confectioners'
2 tablespoons flour	sugar

1 7-inch baked pie shell

Boil sugar and water for 5 minutes. Add cranberries, cook until skins pop open. Beat egg yolks with flour and salt, pour cranberries over mixture. Cook for 2 or 3 minutes, stirring constantly.

Add butter and vanilla. Cool. Fill pie shell, top with meringue of whipped egg whites and confectioners' sugar. Brown in slow oven (300°) 15 minutes.

Steamed Cranberry Pudding

1 cup sifted flour	½ cup brown sugar
2 teaspoons baking powder	⅔ cup finely chopped suet
½ teaspoon salt	1 cup cranberries, chopped
½ cup bread crumbs	⅓ cup milk

Sift flour, baking powder, and salt. Combine bread crumbs, sugar, suet, and cranberries with milk. Add flour mixture. Pour into greased mold, filling only two-thirds full. Cover closely. Place mold on rack in kettle over 1 inch of boiling water. Steam for 2 hours, using high heat at the beginning, and as the steam escapes, lowering the heat for the balance of cooking. Serves 4.

Cranberry Ham Slices

3 cups cranberries	2 slices ham
1½ cups strained honey	(¾ to 1 inch thick)
2 tablespoons whole cloves	

Mix cranberries and honey. Trim ham fat. Place one slice ham in baking dish and cover with cranberry and honey mixture. Top with second slice and cover with remaining cranberry mixture. Stick whole cloves around edge of ham slices, bake in moderate oven (350°) until tender, about 1½ hours. Baste occasionally with liquid in dish. Serves 4.

Cranberry juice is a delightful change as the before-breakfast drink. It also gives additional color and flavor to party punches. Cranberry sauce is delicious with ham, and not to serve it with chicken and turkey is a plain violation of natural law.

Cranberry Sauce

4 cups cranberries   2 cups water

2 cups sugar

Boil water and sugar for 5 minutes. Add cranberries and cook gently, uncovered, without stirring, until thick. Skim. Chill. Serves 8.

Baked Cranberries

2 cups cranberries   1½ cups sugar

Wash cranberries; drain. Put in baking dish. Sprinkle sugar over berries. Cover. Bake in moderate oven (350°) for one hour. Stir once or twice while baking. Chill. Serves 6.

Members of the gourd family will be found contributing beauty and interest to most of the roadside displays. Remarkable, versatile, and sometimes rather eccentric vegetables, they develop every shade of color from pale yellow to brilliant scarlet, and show a unique protean gift, evolving shapes that range from the beautiful to the weird to the humorous. Egocentric gourds with an apparent hankering for fame have more than once appeared in Ripley's "Believe It or Not."

The inedible gourds sell by the millions to people who carry them off for use as ornaments on mantelpiece or

13

hearth, or to be festooned in formations wherever their shapes and colors add to the decorative scheme.

Yankees have always turned these inedible gourds to good use, hollowing them out for use as bottles or vases, or splitting them in half to make excellent scoops. Give the Yankees credit for knowing a good thing when they saw it, but not for invention in this particular case, because gourds have been used as vessels since the most ancient times, and have lent their artistic shapes ("fair attitude!") to other vessels as one can see by even a casual glance at an Egyptian vase or Grecian urn.

Their cousins of the squash branch of the family are equally pleasing to look at, but their good looks are transient; because they make delicious food, their beauty is quickly immolated on the altar of appetite.

Most varieties of squash are delicious when simply boiled in salted water for about thirty minutes, then mashed and seasoned with butter, salt, and pepper. Other ways of preparing it vary the flavor slightly and contribute to menu variety.

Baked Squash

Cut Hubbard squash into 2-inch pieces. Remove seeds and strings. Place in pan. Sprinkle with salt, pepper, brown sugar, and lemon juice. Dot with butter. Cook covered in moderate oven (375°) for half hour. Uncover and cook another half hour, or until tender. Serve the squash in its shell, adding additional butter. Or remove squash from shell, mash, add additional butter, and season to taste.

14

Toasted Squash Seeds

2 cups squash seeds, unwashed   1½ tablespoons melted butter
1½ teaspoons salt

Mix seeds with butter and salt and spread out in shallow pan. Bake in slow oven (275°) until brown, stirring from time to time.
Pumpkin seeds may be toasted in the same way.

Squash Pie

1½ cups squash pulp   1 teaspoon salt
⅔ cup brown sugar   1 teaspoon cinnamon
2 eggs, beaten   ¼ teaspoon nutmeg
1 cup cream   ¼ teaspoon ginger
1 9-inch unbaked pie shell

Combine ingredients. Mix well. Pour into pie shell. Bake in hot oven (425°) for 45 minutes, or longer.

Although Turban, Hubbard, and Butternut are the traditional varieties of squash in New England, many people enjoy Acorn Squash.

Stuffed Acorn Squash

4 acorn squash   1 cup rice, cooked
3 cups chopped ham, cooked   salt and pepper
butter

Cut squash in half, remove seeds and strings. Season with salt and pepper. Dot with butter. Bake in moderate oven (375°) for 30 minutes. Combine ham and rice, moisten with a little milk or cream. Bake additional 10 minutes. Serves 8.

15

Another very versatile member of the gourd family is the pumpkin, appearing, as it has, in such a lowly utilitarian role as a guide for the cutting of hair (hence the expression "punkin head"), also as a most delicious pie filling, and then, upstaging its artistic cousins on at least one night of the year, stepping into a Thespian role with top billing on Halloween!

Pumpkin, like squash, can be boiled with a little butter and spice, and served as a vegetable, but it produces the maximum gustatory excitement when served as a pie.

New England is justly famous for its pies. Newcomers to the section have always been enthusiastic about them.

Pumpkin Chiffon Pie

1 tablespoon gelatine	1½ cups cooked pumpkin
¼ cup cold water	½ teaspoon salt
3 eggs, separated	2 teaspoons cinnamon
½ cup brown sugar	½ teaspoon ginger
½ cup milk	4 tablespoons granulated sugar

1 9-inch baked pie shell

Soften gelatine in water. Beat egg yolks slightly. Add brown sugar, milk, pumpkin, salt, and spices. Cook in double boiler until thick. Stir in the softened gelatine. Chill. Whip egg whites until stiff. When pumpkin mixture begins to set, stir in granulated sugar and fold in the egg whites. Pour into pie shell and chill.

Pumpkin Chiffon Tarts

Use the above recipe and pour mixture into 8 baked and cooled 3-inch tart shells.

Pumpkin Pie

Follow the recipe given on page 15 for squash pie, substituting pumpkin for squash.

Pumpkin Preserve

1 medium-sized pumpkin	½ cup lemon juice
2 cups sugar	6 cups sugar for syrup
	2 cups water for syrup

Cut pumpkin in half, remove seeds, peel off rind. Slice in 1-inch pieces. Pack slices in a crock, alternating layers of pumpkin with layers of sugar. Pour lemon juice over it. Let stand for 2 days. Drain. Make a syrup of sugar and water. Boil pumpkin in this until pieces are very soft. Pour off the syrup, and boil the syrup until thick. Then pour syrup over pumpkin and seal in jars. Makes 4 quarts.

September is the month when we welcome back the prodigal oyster from its long summer vacation. Many of us will be so glad to see oysters again that we'll eat them greedily from the half shell with only a slight squeeze of lemon juice, and perhaps a drop of Tabasco. Then, as the months grow colder, we'll start serving the oysters hot.

Oyster Cocktail Sauce

1 cup catsup	1 tablespoon horse-radish
2 tablespoons lemon juice	1 tablespoon minced celery
¼ teaspoon Tabasco	salt
1 teaspoon vinegar	pepper

Mix ingredients and chill.

Oyster Stew

4 tablespoons butter	2 cups cream
1 quart oysters	1 teaspoon salt
2 cups milk	⅛ teaspoon pepper
pinch of paprika	

Melt butter in pan. Add oysters and cook until edges curl. Combine milk and cream, and bring just to a boil. Add oysters and seasonings. Do not boil. Serves 4.

Scalloped Oysters

½ cup bread crumbs	1 pint oysters, drained
1 cup cracker crumbs	4 tablespoons oyster liquor
¼ cup melted butter	2 cups cream
salt and pepper	

Mix bread crumbs and cracker crumbs. Stir in melted butter. Put a third of the crumbs in bottom of buttered, shallow baking dish. Cover with half the oysters, and sprinkle with salt and pepper. Add half of oyster liquor and half of the cream. Cover with a third of the crumbs, and add remaining oysters, liquor, and cream. Cover with remaining crumbs. Bake 20 minutes in hot oven (450°). Serves 4.

Skewered Oysters

24 large oysters, raw	6 slices bacon
18 fresh mushroom caps	melted butter
6 skewers	

Drain oysters; dry. Wash mushrooms; drain. Cut bacon into 1-inch pieces. Arrange alternately on skewers: 4 oysters, 3 mushrooms, 4 pieces bacon. Brush oysters and mushrooms with butter. Broil in pre-heated broiler 4 inches from heat. Turn once. Serve when mushrooms are tender and bacon is crisp. Serves 6.

Oyster-Ham Sandwich

12 oysters, raw	bread crumbs
pepper	3 slices ham, broiled
melted butter	toast

Dry oysters; season. Dip in butter and bread crumbs. Broil until golden. Serve with ham and toast. Serves 3.

Chicken Smothered in Oysters

2 young chickens, quartered	2 cups milk
salt and pepper	1 quart oysters
½ cup butter	2 cups cream

Clean and quarter chickens. Season with salt and pepper. Sauté for a few minutes in butter, then place in baking dish. Pour some of the butter into dish, and add milk. Cover and bake in moderate oven (350°) for one hour, basting frequently. Add oysters and cream. Cook another 15 minutes. Pour oysters and cream around the chicken and serve. Serves 8.

Like September's oysters, October's scallops are delicious. Most of the nation is supplied by the New Bedford fleet. They taste good prepared in the simplest possible way: just rolled in salted and peppered bread crumbs, and fried or broiled. Three or four minutes on each side will be about right.

Scallops in Wine

3 cups scallops	2 tablespoons flour
1½ cups dry white wine	¼ cup cream
2 tablespoons butter, melted	¼ teaspoon curry powder

salt and pepper

Wash and drain scallops. Bring wine to a boil and add scallops. Simmer for 8 minutes. Put liquor aside. Blend flour and butter, and add to liquor. Bring liquor to a boil, then turn down heat and add cream, curry powder, salt, and pepper. Cut scallops into small pieces and add to mixture. Heat thoroughly. Serves 4.

Scallops Casino

Cut scallops into small pieces and place in scallop shells. Sprinkle with salt and pepper. Cover each with strip of bacon. Bake in hot oven (400°) for 15 minutes. Serve with melted butter.

Scallops Vinaigrette

16 scallops	¾ cup olive oil
2 cups boiled potatoes, sliced	¼ cup vinegar
¼ cup finely chopped onion	salt and pepper
¼ cup finely chopped parsley	1 teaspoon chopped dill

Simmer scallops for 5 minutes in salt water to cover. Drain and cool scallops. Cut scallops in quarters and combine with sliced potatoes. Combine olive oil, vinegar, onion, parsley, and seasoning. Mix with scallops and potatoes. Sprinkle with dill. Serves 4.

Nantucket Scallop Chowder

2 onions, sliced	2 cups boiling water
4 tablespoons butter	1 cup potatoes, diced
1 pint scallops	4 cups scalded milk

salt and pepper

Sauté onions in butter. Remove onions from pan. Cut up scallops and sauté in butter. Add onions, scallops, and potatoes to boiling water. Simmer for 30 minutes. Add scalded milk and simmer additional 15 minutes. Add seasoning. Serves 5.

Soup has its own special merits for fortifying one against the chilly weather, and many a New England family keeps a kettleful simmering on the stove. September's vegetables are used in all of the favorite Yankee soups.

Vermont Cabbage Soup

3 cups cabbage, chopped fine	3 cups milk
1½ cups water	1 cup cream

salt and pepper

Cook cabbage in water for about 15 minutes. Add milk and cream. Season with salt and pepper. Serve hot. Serves 4.

Stockpot

Put into a stockpot all odd scraps of meat, cooked and uncooked, which cannot be used otherwise; pieces of skin; bones (chopped into small pieces), cooked or uncooked. Cover with plenty of water, simmer slowly but steadily beside the fire. This should furnish material for sauces and soup. Pieces of bread, cold vegetables, remains of sauces, etc., should be used up to thicken and flavor it. In winter the stockpot should be entirely cleared out once a week, and in summer twice a week.

—from an old cook book—

Vegetable Chowder

2 cups celery, diced	6 cups water
2 onions, diced	1 cup cooked green beans
2 carrots, diced	1 cup tomatoes
1 cup shredded lettuce leaves	salt and pepper

Sauté celery, onions, carrots, and lettuce in butter for about 10 minutes. Add to kettle of boiling water. Add beans, tomatoes, salt, and pepper. Simmer for 30 minutes. Serves 5.

Split Pea Soup

2 cups dried split peas	2 potatoes, diced
12 cups water	1½ cups chopped celery
1 ham bone	1 clove garlic
1 onion, chopped	salt and pepper

Soak peas overnight. Drain the peas, reserving the liquid for cooking. Place peas in kettle, adding liquid and additional cold water to make 12 cups in all. Add ham bone and simmer for 4 hours covered. In the last half hour of cooking, add vegetables and seasonings. Put soup through a sieve and serve. Serves 8.

Boston Black Bean Soup

2 cups dried black beans	⅛ teaspoon black pepper
1 tablespoon salt	⅛ teaspoon dry mustard
2 quarts water	1 cup cream
2 tablespoons butter	6 thin slices of lemon
2 tablespoons flour	6 cloves
1 tablespoon minced onion	1 hard-boiled egg

22

Cover beans with water and soak overnight. In the morning, drain, add salt and water, and cook for two hours, until beans are soft. Press beans through sieve, then simmer additional 15 to 20 minutes. Melt butter in saucepan, gradually adding flour, onion, pepper, mustard, and cream. Stir until slightly thick, then add to bean purée. Heat just to boiling point. In each bowl place slice of lemon with clove and slice of hard-boiled egg. Serves 6.

Daniel Webster prided himself on making a good fish chowder, and here in his own words is the recipe.

Daniel Webster's Fish Chowder

"Take a cod of ten pounds, well cleaned, leaving on the skin. Cut into pieces one and a half pounds thick, preserving the head whole. Take one and a half pounds of clear, fat salt pork, cut in thin slices. Do the same with twelve potatoes. Take the largest pot you have. Try out the pork first, then take out pieces of pork, leaving drippings in. Add to that three parts of water, a layer of fish, so as to cover bottom of pot; next a layer of potatoes, then two tablespoons of salt, one teaspoon of pepper, then the pork, another layer of fish and remainder of the potatoes. Fill the pot with water to cover the ingredients. Put over a good fire. Let the chowder boil twenty-five minutes. When this is done have a quart of boiling milk ready, and ten hard crackers split and dipped in cold water. Add milk and crackers. Let the whole boil five minutes. The chowder is then ready to be first-rate if you have followed the directions. An onion may be added if you like the flavor."

Typical New England dinners take on size and substance to meet the demands of the weather.

Yankee Pot Roast

4 pounds beef	5 or 6 raisins
Salt, pepper, flour	1 small turnip, sliced
⅛ pound salt pork	6 carrots
1 bay leaf	6 onions
sprig parsley	6 potatoes

Wipe meat with clean damp cloth. Sprinkle with salt, pepper, and flour. Fry a small piece of salt pork in an iron pot. Put in meat and brown on all sides. When brown, add enough boiling water to cover bottom of pot. Add bay leaf, parsley, and raisins. Cover and simmer slowly for 3 hours, keeping about 1 cup of water under the meat. The last hour of cooking add carrots, onions, turnip; add potatoes the last half hour. Serve on a platter with the vegetables arranged around the meat. Mix 2 tablespoons flour in ¼ cup cold water to a smooth paste to thicken the gravy. Serves 6.

A great New England favorite is the boiled dinner, traditionally served on Mondays and Wednesdays throughout the fall and winter.

New England Boiled Dinner

5 pounds brisket corned beef	6 carrots, unpeeled
4 peppercorns	1 small cabbage, quartered
6 small beets, unpeeled	8 peeled potatoes
4 medium-sized turnips, peeled	

Place meat in kettle with peppercorns. Cover with cold water. Simmer 3½ to 4 hours, until meat is tender. During last hour of cooking, remove peppercorns and add beets, turnips, carrots. In last half hour, add cabbage and potatoes. When ready to serve, remove skins from beets. Serves 8.

Red Flannel Hash

1 cup chopped, cooked corned beef	½ cup chopped onion
1 cup chopped, cooked beets	1 tablespoon drippings
3 cups chopped, boiled potatoes	1 tablespoon cream
	1 tablespoon butter

Chop ingredients on wooden board or in wooden bowl. (Moisten with stock if necessary.) Put drippings in pan, and add corned beef and vegetables. Brown slowly. When almost ready, add cream and butter. Give final browning and serve. Serves 4.

Creamed Beef Bacon

1 pound beef bacon, sliced	2 tablespoons flour
1 quart boiling water	3 cups light cream
2 tablespoons butter	salt and pepper

Soak beef bacon in boiling water for 15 or 20 minutes; then drain. Make cream sauce by melting butter, stirring in flour, and gradually adding cream. Heat thoroughly. Add beef and seasoning. Cook over low flame for 15 minutes. Serve on toast. Serves 6.

Dried Beef

½ pound dried beef	4 tablespoons flour
4 tablespoons butter	2 cups milk

Pour boiling water on the beef; drain and dry. Sauté beef in butter. Remove beef from pan and add flour to the butter. Cook until brown, then pour in milk, stirring constantly until mixture thickens. Add the beef, and serve. Serves 5.

Boiled Beef Tongue

1 3-pound fresh beef tongue   6 peppercorns
1 onion, peeled   1 teaspoon salt
1 carrot, peeled   parsley
          1 cup celery, including leaves

Cover the tongue with boiling water and simmer with the above
ingredients until it is tender, about 2½ hours. Drain. Skin the
tongue. Serve hot or cold. Serves 12.

Yankees have always been pleased with baked beans for
the same reasons that we are today: they make an appetizing
meal in themselves, they team up with any kind of meat,
they are very filling and nourishing, and, once made, can
be served at several meals.

Our pious forebears started their Sabbath on Saturday
night, which meant keeping all labor, including cooking, at
the irreducible minimum all day Sunday. It was quickly
found that beans seemed designed by Nature to fit this situation. They were soaked Friday night, cooked all day Saturday, served for Saturday night supper, for Sunday breakfast,
and all day Sunday.

Boston Baked Beans

1 quart pea beans   ⅓ cup molasses
½ pound salt pork   1 teaspoon salt
⅓ cup sugar   ½ teaspoon dry mustard
          boiling water

Wash and pick over beans. Soak overnight in cold water. In
the morning, drain, cover beans with fresh water, and simmer
26

until skins break. Put beans into bean pot. Score pork and press into beans, filling pot until three-fourths full. Add sugar, molasses, salt, and mustard. Cover with boiling water. Cover and bake 8 hours without stirring in slow oven (250°). Keep the beans almost covered but not swimming in water. Remove cover during last half hour of baking. Serves 8.

One breakfast custom from which no true Bostonian would think of departing was the serving of codfish balls, baked beans, and brown bread on Sunday morning.

Codfish Balls

1½ cups salt cod	2 tablespoons butter
2½ cups potatoes	1 egg
	pepper

Soak fish in water half an hour. Drain and flake it. Boil with potatoes until potatoes are tender. Drain. Put back on fire momentarily to dry completely. Mash the mixture, add butter and pepper. Beat until fluffy. Add egg and continue beating. Drop mixture by tablespoonfuls into deep hot fat (375°). Fry until golden brown. Drain. Serves 6.

Boston Brown Bread

1 cup rye flour	1 teaspoon soda
1 cup yellow corn meal	¾ cup molasses
1 cup graham flour	2 cups sour milk
1 teaspoon salt	1 cup raisins

Mix and sift dry ingredients. Dissolve soda in small quantity of water and stir into molasses. Combine with sour milk, then mix

27

into the dry ingredients. Flour the raisins and add to the mixture. Mix thoroughly and pour into two greased molds, filling two-thirds to top. The cover should be tight-fitting, and should be buttered before being placed on the mold. It should then be tied down with a string so that the bread will not force off the cover as it rises. Place molds on racks in kettle containing boiling water which comes halfway up around molds. Cover and steam for 3 hours, adding more boiling water if needed. To cut brown bread, use a string.

Frugal Pie

Required: ½ pound cold meat; 1 pound cold potatoes; 2 small onions; 1 sprig flavoring herb; 1 teaspoonful flour; 1 ounce dripping; 1 tablespoonful milk; 1 teacupful cold water or pot liquor; ¼ teaspoonful pepper; ¼ teaspoonful salt.

Cut the meat into thin slanting slices, with the grain, not against it. Skin, scald, and slice the onions, and brown them slightly with half of the dripping in a pan; pour away the dripping; break the flour with a little cold water; add it with the rest of the water, the sprig of herb, salt, and pepper to the onions. Simmer till the onion is tender, about one quarter of an hour, stirring to prevent the flour sticking to the pan. Remove the sprig; let the sauce cool; pour it into a pie-dish; place the pieces of meat in it. Mash the potatoes; add the milk and the other half of the dripping to them. Lay the potatoes smoothly on the top of the meat; score them across with a knife. Put the pie into the oven to brown; when browned, it is ready. If there is no oven, place the pie on the hob or hot plate for a few minutes to warm through, but do not allow it to boil; then brown it in front of the fire. The top of the pie may be glazed by brushing it over with a little milk before cooking.

—from an old cook book—

Hasty Pudding has been one of the mainstays of the Yankee diet for centuries, served as a breakfast dish, as the entree for supper, as a vegetable with meat at dinnertime, and as a dessert. The earliest Colonists in this country learned how to make it from the Indians.

Given its name because it can be prepared so quickly and easily, hasty pudding is also known by the less appetizing name "Corn Meal Mush."

Hasty Pudding

4 cups boiling water   1 cup corn meal
1 teaspoon salt

Put salt in water and bring to a boil. Slowly add corn meal, stirring constantly. Cook for 30 minutes in pan or for one hour in double boiler. Serve in bowls with plenty of rich milk and butter. Add any one of the following: molasses, honey, maple syrup, maple sugar. Serves 4.

This was *the* breakfast food before the packaged ones were developed. It can also be poured into a bread or cake pan (rinsed with cold water), refrigerated, and then sliced for frying with bacon.

Now is the time when Maine's Aroostook County is in the throes of getting in its potato crop, even closing the schools in some communities so that the children can help with the harvest.

Fresh from the ground, these potatoes are unusually good

and tempt us to look up all of our potato recipes. Harvesters find an occasional slice of raw potato refreshing, and bits of the raw vegetable add crispness to a tossed salad.

One of the many picturesque features of Maine county fairs is the potato wagon surrounded by bags of the newly dug spuds. Peeled and sliced while you wait, the potatoes are french-fried, and many Down Easters prefer eating them with just a sprinkling of vinegar.

Aroostook Savory Supper

Line the bottom of buttered baking dish with raw, sliced onions. Fill dish with thin slices of raw Maine potatoes. Add salt and pepper. Add water to almost cover. Put cubes of salt pork on top. Cook slowly 3 hours in slow oven (250°).

Mashed Mainers with Mint

Boil Maine potatoes in jackets. Remove jackets. Mash potatoes. Add salt, butter, hot milk. Beat until fluffy. Add 2 tablespoons finely chopped fresh mint leaves.

A baked Maine potato with butter, salt, and pepper can hardly be improved upon, but baked stuffed potatoes are delicious, too, and add variety to the menu.

Baked Stuffed Maine Potatoes

6 large potatoes, baked   1½ tablespoons butter
½ cup minced leeks   ½ cup cream, warm
                    salt and pepper

Scoop out insides of potatoes. Sauté leeks in butter. Combine with cream and seasoning. Add to potatoes. Replace potato stuffing in skins and put back in oven to heat and brown. Serves 6.

HERB STUFFING

2 tablespoons basil	3 tablespoons butter, melted
2 tablespoons tarragon	½ cup cream, warm
2 tablespoons parsley	salt and pepper
grated Parmesan cheese	

Mix herbs with butter. Add cream and seasoning. Combine with potatoes. Replace potato stuffing in skins. Top with grated Parmesan cheese. Bake in hot oven (450°) until brown. Serves 6.

Hot Potato Salad

8 medium-sized potatoes	¼ cup chicken stock or water
5 strips minced bacon	½ cup vinegar
⅓ cup chopped onion	½ teaspoon sugar
⅓ cup chopped celery	½ teaspoon salt
1 cup chopped dill pickle	⅛ teaspoon paprika
¼ teaspoon dry mustard	

Cook potatoes in skins until tender. Peel and slice potatoes while hot. In a skillet, heat minced bacon. Add onion, celery, pickle, and sauté until onion is golden brown. In a separate saucepan, heat stock or water, vinegar, sugar, salt, paprika, and mustard to boiling point. Pour into the skillet with the onion, celery, and pickle. Combine this mixture with potatoes and serve at once with chopped parsley or chives. Serves 8.

Cold Potato Salad

4 cups boiled potatoes, diced
2 hard-boiled eggs, sliced
1 onion, minced
½ cup olives, chopped
½ cup celery, diced

¼ cup celery leaves, minced
½ cup sweet pickles, diced
½ cup cucumbers, diced
salt and pepper
paprika

1½ cups mayonnaise

Mix all ingredients. Just before serving, sprinkle with paprika.
Serves 8-10.

Chapter 2   FALL

October 21–December 1

THERE are many ancient superstitions and weather sayings that apply to late October. "Rain in October, much snow in March." "A dry October, and February will have many blizzards." About all one can decide from these is that occasions of extremes have always been present. If adages are unreliable, neither is there any scientific way of knowing what a given season will bring.

There are those who swear by the beavers and the poplar trees as sources of valuable weather hints. If they see these industrious little animals felling the trees for dams as well as food, they foresee a drought or dry spell. With plenty of rain ahead, the beavers won't worry too much about new dams and will leave the larger trees alone.

Then there are the sayings about squirrels' tails and the thickness of the pig's melt bone. Each, we say, unto his own idea of what these things may mean. Ours is that animals are wonderful adjusters to climate as they find it, but for predicting or preparing for what may be ahead they are not too adept. Come an early snow and they'll be caught in it just as flat as we will.

> "No warmth nor cheer nor ease,
> No comfortable feel in any member,
> No shade, no shine, no butterflies, or bees,
> No fruits, no flowers, no leaves, no birds, No-vember."

This is the way the Englishman Thomas Hood saw this month and, if indeed we are to accept the inevitable and crawl away into our holes the way hibernating animals are doing, it will be this way for us, too.

But not us—for we have heard a whirring in the dry leaves and know that partridge, pheasant, and woodcock hunting is at its best. We'll ramble over hill and dale with gun and dog, and hope not to come home emptyhanded.

"By St. Martin's Day [November 11] winter is well on its way." So goes the old saying. There is no denying that by now a reverse process of nature has set in. The earth, instead of losing heat to the atmosphere, has begun to take cold in. No longer do sullen mists appear in the valleys of morning and evening. The day or night is either good or bad and no mist about it.

A study of the ground at this time of year is one to which only a few have paid much attention. There are, of course,

34

numerous estimates as to how far the frost will penetrate the surface of the earth during the coming winter. But when one considers that most of our climate in New England depends on the direct reaction of our soils to the rays of the sun, it is surprising that more is not made of such a study.

There are numerous facts and figures available about how the forest floor of leaves acts as a blanket or insulation, how black will absorb more heat than white, how a grass-covered field is less liable to frost action than an open one. We all know how some protection for rose bushes and perennial plants against winter's thawing and freezing of the ground is necessary. And here is this fascinating deepening of the frost into the ground almost by tenths of inches—ever, as the earth continues its tilting away from the sun, deeper, deeper, deeper.

It is said the ground hog plans to be awakened, come February 2, when this frost has reached him deep in his hole to tell him the pendulum has swung the other way and it is time to get up and look around.

Possibly four—we have heard as much as six—feet is as deep as the frost will go. So here we have an outside coating of frozen earth from four to six feet deep which, we might say, really makes our winter.

But how come, one may ask, that even with the frost a foot or two deep in the ground only the small ponds are frozen over? At a time when all of our extremities are just about numb, the big lakes go merrily on as open and as joyously free as they ever were in summer!

The lakes will not freeze over until all of the waters in

them have reached a uniform temperature of thirty-nine degrees. The first cold snap will bring the surface of the lake down to such a level, but the warmer water will then rise from below to replace that which has been cooled. Such a cooling process has to be repeated many times before a lake many hundreds of feet deep will be ready to freeze. If there is a stratification of weeds below the surface, a time will come when, warmer and thus lighter than the waters above them, all of these will rise to the surface to make an island never seen before.

Well-fortified and comparatively free from danger, the modern family is given an opportunity to enjoy the romance and poetry of New England's fall storms. By the sea, particularly, one may hear in waves and wind, as do the Welsh at such times, the ringing of the bells of steeples long since buried under advancing waters. And what is more relaxing and wonderful than the raindrops on tent or cabin roof? When the wind begins to roar instead of whistle through the treetops and great oaks are uprooted in the forest is a time to consider the power and greatness of natural forces—and how often these forces come to help man instead of hurt him. No "Pollyanna" thinking, this—for ignorant as we are about the causes of weather, even the tiniest living thing recognizes a wholly integrated annual cycle of existence: night becomes day, fall becomes winter. After the rain comes sunshine; from January 1 it is only one hundred days to the first bluebird. The great storms have their usefulness in this general cyclical scheme of things—even as do the good days for golf or bathing.

About the middle of November come the first real snows.

Thanksgiving, often white, marks the end of fall. The snows, as a rule, don't remain for long, but only the foolish will disregard the shortening days, bleak trees, and scurrying clouds. Winter is in the offing.

With these phenomena of nature going on all around us, it almost goes without saying that we, too, must react in various ways to this swing toward the winter period.

* * *

Among the most exciting seasonal phenomena is the ripening of the late apples: trees in the orchard grow heavier and heavier with luscious fruit. It becomes both our pleasure and our responsibility to make the most of this abundance.

Apple Pie

6 medium-sized tart apples	1 9-inch pie shell and crust
1 cup brown sugar	2 tablespoons butter
1 tablespoon cornstarch	½ tablespoon lemon juice
¼ teaspoon cinnamon	½ teaspoon vanilla
⅛ teaspoon nutmeg	2 tablespoons cream

Pare, core, and thinly slice the apples. Combine sugar, cornstarch, and spices. Stir the apples in this mixture until well coated. Place in pie shell, gently rounding at the edges. Dot with butter. Sprinkle with lemon juice and vanilla. Moisten edges of crust and cover pie with top crust. Press and crimp edges. Gloss crust with cream and sprinkle lightly with sugar and cinnamon. Bake in hot oven (450°) for 20 minutes. Reduce heat to 350° and bake 40 minutes longer.

Baked Apples

4 apples   2 teaspoons butter
4 tablespoons brown sugar   2 teaspoons cinnamon
                grated lemon rind

Core apples without removing stem end. Place in baking dish
with 1 tablespoon of water for each apple. Fill centers with sugar,
butter, cinnamon, and lemon rind. Cook in a hot oven (425°),
basting frequently, for 40 minutes, or until tender. Serve with
cream. Serves 4.

Apple Pan Dowdy

3 cups apples, sliced   ¼ teaspoon cinnamon
3 tablespoons sugar   ¼ teaspoon salt
3 tablespoons molasses   butter
¼ teaspoon nutmeg   biscuit dough

Place apples in buttered baking dish. Add mixture of sugar,
molasses, spices, and salt. Dot with butter. Bake in moderate
(375°) oven for 30 minutes. Then cover with a rich biscuit dough,
spreading it out to edge of dish. Put back in oven and bake for
20 minutes. Serve with cream. Serves 4.

Apple Dumplings

2 cups sifted flour   ¾ cup milk
2½ teaspoons baking powder   8 apples
½ teaspoon salt   8 tablespoons sugar
½ cup shortening   4 tablespoons butter
                cinnamon

Sift flour, baking powder, and salt. Cut in shortening. Add milk
and stir. Knead lightly on floured board. Roll ⅛-inch thick.
Divide dough in 8 parts. Pare and core apples, and place one
apple on each section of dough. Fill hollow of each apple with 1
38

tablespoon sugar and 1 teaspoon butter. Fold dough over apple, pressing edges together. Place in shallow pan, sprinkle with cinnamon and sugar. Dot with butter. Bake in moderate oven (400°) for 30-40 minutes. Serve with cream. Serves 8.

Apples and Pork Chops

4 pork chops, 1-inch thick 1 cup cream, heated
1 cup apples, halved   salt and pepper
½ cup brown sugar   paprika

Sear the chops and season with salt and paprika. Place apples over the chops, skin side down. Cover apples with brown sugar. Cover bottom of pan with hot cream. Cover pan and bake chops in moderate oven (350°) for 40 minutes. Add salt and pepper. Baste frequently. Serves 4.

Apples and Ham

3 ham slices, ¼-inch thick 2 tablespoons brown sugar
3 Greenings, sliced and peeled 3 teaspoons lemon juice

Arrange alternate layers of ham and apples in buttered baking dish. Sprinkle apples with brown sugar; sprinkle top layer of apples with lemon juice. Bake in covered dish in moderate oven (375°) for 40 minutes, removing cover for last 10 minutes of cooking. Serves 3.

Apples and Sausage

6 large apples, cored   1 teaspoon salt
1 cup sausage meat   2 tablespoons brown sugar

Select tart apples. Remove pulp. Chop and combine with sausage meat. Sprinkle inside of apples with salt and brown sugar, then fill with sausage mixture. Bake in moderate (375°) oven until tender. Serves 6.

Its delicate blend of tart and sweet makes applesauce delightful at every meal of the day: in place of fruit juice at breakfast time or served with bacon; in combination with ham or pork for luncheon or dinner; and as the principal ingredient in a galaxy of desserts.

Applesauce

Wash and core McIntosh apples. Cut into quarters, place in saucepan, and barely cover with water. Add a pinch of salt and sugar. Cook for 3 minutes. Strain.

Applesauce Cake

1 teaspoon baking soda	½ cup butter
1 tablespoon warm water	1 teaspoon vanilla
1 cup applesauce, unsweetened	½ cup molasses
½ cup sugar	2 cups flour, sifted
½ teaspoon ground cloves	½ teaspoon salt
½ teaspoon cinnamon	½ cup seedless raisins, chopped
¼ teaspoon nutmeg	½ cup walnuts

Dissolve soda in water and stir into applesauce. Mix sugar and spices. Cream sugar mixture and butter. Stir in applesauce and vanilla. Add molasses, then stir in flour sifted with salt, raisins, and walnuts. Bake in greased 9-inch tube pan in moderate oven (350°) for 40 minutes.

Applesauce Cream

2 cups cream	½ teaspoon almond extract
2 cups applesauce	grated chocolate

Whip the cream until stiff. Fold in applesauce and almond extract. Sprinkle top with grated chocolate. Chill and serve. Serves 6.

Apple Cider

Gushing fresh from the press, cider is delicious and wholesome, and in almost every New England community there is a cider press capable of supplying the needs of a large area. As autumn comes along, we watch for the familiar roadside signs: "Apple cider!"
Traditionally, cider is served in New England with

Spiced Doughnuts

2 eggs, beaten	4 cups flour
1 cup sugar	4 teaspoons baking powder
1 cup milk	¼ teaspoon cinnamon
5 tablespoons shortening,	¼ teaspoon nutmeg
melted	¼ teaspoon ground cloves
½ teaspoon salt	

Add sugar, milk, and shortening to beaten eggs. Sift flour before measuring, then resift with baking powder, spices, and salt. Combine the egg mixture with flour mixture. Stir until blended. Roll dough ¼-inch thick and cut into desired shapes. Fry in deep fat heated to 375° about 3 minutes, first on one side, then the other. Sprinkle with sugar. Yield: 30 doughnuts.

Cider Champagne

For those who would like to ferment a quantity of cider for winter use, the process is fairly simple, but should be followed exactly.
First, be sure that the cider is pressed from sound, freshly gathered apples that have not been frozen. First and last, the

41

cider should be kept in a cool place, and the middle of November is a good time to process it.

Secure a new whisky barrel, and let's call it a ten-gallon barrel just for the sake of establishing correct proportions. Funnel in cider until almost full. Then add two pounds of white sugar and two pounds of light brown sugar. Leave out the bung while the cider is working, but cover the hole with a piece of cloth or burlap. Watch to make sure that the barrel is kept full, adding additional cider from time to time. After about two months it will stop working and be ready to bottle. Syphon it off from the top, avoiding sediment.

Foodwise, our attitudes are affected at this time of year by the fact that the harvest is in, the hunting season comes along, and then Thanksgiving, just as in the days of the Pilgrims:

"Our harvest being gotten in, our Governor sente four men out fowling that so we might, after a more special manner, rejoyce together after we had gathered the fruit of our labours. These four, in one day, killed as much fowl as, with a little help besides, served the company almost a week, at which time, amongst other recreations, we exercised our armes, many of the Indians coming amongst us. And amongst the rest, their greatest King, Massasoit, with some ninety men, whom, for three days, we entertained and feasted. And they went out and killed five deer, which they brought to the Plantation, and bestowed on our Governor and upon the Captaine and others...." (This being a quotation from a letter written by Edward Winslow to a friend in England.)

Down through the three centuries since then, New England men in large numbers have relied on their rifles and shotguns to furnish their tables with duck, goose, grouse, pheasant, quail, deer, and an occasional bear. The women have learned at an early age to bring the men's bag to the table in the form of a feast, and their recipes have met the dinnertime test of generations of men.

Roast Wild Duck

Singe, clean, and draw the duck. Stuff with sliced apple, chopped celery, a small amount of raw potato. Freeze overnight. Discard the stuffing. Have duck at room temperature. Dry thoroughly inside and out. Rub inside with salt. Fill cavity loosely with peeled and chopped apples and raisins. Brush with butter and place in uncovered roasting pan in moderate oven (325°). For rare duck, roast 10 to 12 minutes to the pound; 15-20 minutes, well done. Baste frequently with fat in the pan, to which you may add dry red wine. Serve with cranberries or orange slices.

Barbecued Wild Duck

Clean duck. Split into halves. Dry thoroughly. Cook under the broiler until brown, basting frequently with this sauce:

4 teaspoons lemon juice	1 teaspoon tomato catsup
1 teaspoon Worcestershire sauce	1 clove garlic, mashed
	1 tablespoon butter
1 tablespoon brown sugar	

Before serving, sprinkle duck with salt and paprika.

43

Braised Wild Duck

wild duck	1 carrot, sliced
lemon juice	1 teaspoon parsley
salt and pepper	⅛ teaspoon thyme
4 slices bacon	4 tablespoons brown sugar
1 onion, sliced	2 tablespoons orange juice
grated lemon peel	

Clean and disjoint duck. Rub pieces with lemon juice. Season with salt and pepper. Place in skillet with bacon, onion, carrot, parsley, and thyme. Sear until it begins to brown, then reduce heat, drain fat, and sprinkle duck with brown sugar, orange juice, and grated lemon peel. Cover and braise over moderate heat for about 30 minutes. Serve.

Roast Grouse

Clean the birds, dry thoroughly. Stuff and place in roaster. Cook in slow oven (300°) until done, allowing about 45 minutes total cooking time, since grouse is served rare. Cover the breast well with bacon slices; when done, remove bacon and brush the bird with butter. Then dredge lightly with flour and put in hot oven (450°) until brown. Grouse may be stuffed with any of the following:

> braised onions and celery
> sauerkraut soaked in dry wine
> celery and cranberries
> celery, onion, apple, and butter

Broiled Grouse

Clean, split, and draw birds. Dust lightly with flour. Place breast down on broiler rack under moderate heat (350°). Broil 15 to

44

20 minutes, turning once. Baste frequently with melted butter. Season with salt and pepper. Serve on toast with drippings.

Broiled Pheasant

Pheasant may be broiled in the same way as grouse, allowing 30 to 40 minutes for broiling.

Pan-Broiled Pheasant

Clean and split down the back. Season with salt and pepper. Brush with melted butter. Roll in flour and place in open roasting pan. Put several pieces of salt pork in the pan. Roast for 30 minutes in hot (400°) oven. Baste often.

Broiled Quail

Quail may be broiled in the same way as grouse.

Quail on Skewers

Clean the birds. Rub inside with salt and pepper. Pin bacon strips around the quail with toothpicks and place on skewers just over the fire. Turn frequently over hot fire to sear. Then reduce heat and broil slowly for 15 minutes.

Quail on Toast

Clean the birds. Rub inside with salt. Sprinkle outside with salt, pepper, and flour. Brown quail in melted butter in skillet. Then add small quantity of water and mushrooms. Cover and cook over low heat for 10 minutes. Add chopped parsley, cook until tender. Serve on buttered toast.

45

Fried Rabbit

1 young rabbit	flour
salt and pepper	2 tablespoons milk
orégano	1 egg, beaten

Cut rabbit in serving pieces. Season. Dip pieces in flour, then in milk and egg mixture. Roll again in flour and fry in deep hot fat. Brown, then reduce heat and cook for 30 minutes, or until tender. Serves 2.

Smothered Rabbit

Cut rabbit in serving pieces. Salt and pepper. Dust with flour. Brown well in butter. Place in casserole. Cover meat with onion slices and thick sour cream. Cook in moderate (350°) oven until done.

Rabbit Stew

Clean rabbit and soak overnight in water, slightly salted. In the morning, cover with fresh cold water and simmer for an hour. Add onions, potatoes, and other vegetables, salt and pepper, and simmer for about 50 minutes, or until tender.

Venison Marinade

1 cup boiling water	½ teaspoon hyssop
¾ cup vinegar	½ teaspoon tarragon
2 bay leaves	1 teaspoon pepper
4 cloves	½ teaspoon salt
2 onions, chopped	¼ teaspoon nutmeg
1 clove garlic, crushed	

Combine ingredients in order given and use as marinade for Venison Stew.

Venison Stew

4 pounds venison shoulder or brisket	2 cups celery, chopped
3 tablespoons bacon fat	3 tomatoes
½ pound salt pork	1 green pepper, diced
4 potatoes	1¼ tablespoons tarragon vinegar
2 onions	1 clove garlic
4 carrots	½ teaspoon marigold

Cut meat into 1½-inch cubes. Marinate for 24 hours. Drain. Sear meat in bacon fat. Place in kettle and cover with cold water. Add salt pork, cut into small pieces. Cook until tender, about 2 hours. Add vegetables and seasonings. Simmer for 45-50 minutes. Serves 8.

Stuffed Venison Shoulder

venison shoulder	⅛ teaspoon pepper
rosemary	1 carrot
1 cup chopped ham	1 onion, chopped
1 cup bread crumbs	½ cup mushrooms
½ teaspoon salt	1 clove garlic, crushed
1 cup white wine	

Bone the shoulder. Rub lightly with crushed dried rosemary. Stuff shoulder with combined ham, bread crumbs, salt, and pepper. Sew the shoulder. Braise carrot, onion, mushrooms, garlic, and wine. Cook until tender in moderate oven (300°), allowing 30 minutes to the pound.

Broiled Venison Chops

Brush chops with olive oil. Season with salt and pepper. Sear under the broiler for 15 seconds on each side. Brush chops again with olive oil and broil 2 to 3 minutes on each side.

Deer Loaf

1 pound ground venison	1 cup stale white bread
½ pound pork sausage meat	crumbs
6 teaspoons chopped onion	1 egg, slightly beaten
1 green pepper, diced	2 tablespoons parsley, chopped
1 clove garlic, peeled and	2 tomatoes, peeled and diced
chopped	½ cup water
1 carrot, diced	2 teaspoons Worcestershire
2 cups celery, chopped	sauce

Sauté onion, pepper, and garlic. Combine venison and pork sausage with all ingredients except the last three. Shape into a meat loaf, place in roasting pan. Cover with tomatoes, water, and Worcestershire sauce. Bake for 1½ hours in moderate (375°) oven. Serves 4.

Bear Marinade

2 cups cider	1 teaspoon paprika
¼ cup orange juice	1 clove garlic, crushed
1 tablespoon lemon juice	¼ teaspoon hyssop
1 onion, chopped	1 bay leaf
1 carrot, diced	½ teaspoon mustard
2 cups celery, diced	⅛ teaspoon nutmeg

Combine ingredients and bring to a boil. Boil for 5 minutes. Marinate meat for 5 hours.

Roast Bear

Marinate bear loin. Place in hot oven (450°) for 10 minutes. Reduce heat to moderate (350°) oven and cook 20 minutes to the pound, basting often with bear marinade.

Bradford, in his famous history of the Pilgrims, speaks of the hungry days and then of an improvement in their situation: "And now began to come in store of foule, as winter approached.... And besides waterfoule, there was great store of wild turkies, of which they tooke many...."

Wild turkeys have been replaced by the domestic variety, raised on turkey farms the length and breadth of New England—with a particular concentration in Rhode Island. Preparation of the turkeys for the table has changed little because young girls have learned the recipes at their mothers' elbows.

Roast Turkey

1 12-pound turkey

Rinse turkey, inside and out, with cold water. Dry with a cloth. Rub well on the inside with salt. Fill loosely with dressing, tie up the bird, and place in roasting pan with the breast up. Brush the breast, legs, and wings with melted fat. Place a thick layer of fat on the bird and cover with a cloth. Roast uncovered in a slow oven (300°) until done, allowing about 20 minutes to the pound. Baste every half hour. Remove cloth during last 20 minutes of cooking. Serves 12.

Chestnut Stuffing

4 cups chestnuts	1 cup cream
½ cup melted butter	6 cups bread crumbs
2 teaspoons salt	4 tablespoons chopped parsley
¾ teaspoon pepper	2 cups chopped celery

½ cup grated onion

Boil chestnuts until soft, put through potato ricer, and combine with balance of ingredients. Yield: stuffing for 10-12-pound bird.

Apricot-Prune Stuffing

1½ cups dried apricots
1½ cups dried prunes
4 cups rice, cooked
6 tablespoons melted butter
⅓ cup chopped parsley

1 cup chopped celery
⅓ cup chopped onion
¼ teaspoon thyme
¼ teaspoon clove
salt and pepper

Soak apricots and prunes for an hour. Drain. Combine rice, butter, parsley, celery, and onion. Add apricots and prunes. Mix lightly with a fork. Add seasonings. Chill before using. Yield: stuffing for 10-12-pound bird.

Celery-Bread Stuffing

6 cups stale bread crumbs
2 cups cornbread crumbs
2 small onions, chopped fine
3 cups celery, chopped
½ cup parsley
1 apple, chopped fine

¼ teaspoon pepper
2½ teaspoons salt
½ teaspoon thyme
½ teaspoon sage
1½ cups turkey stock
½ cup butter, melted

3 eggs, beaten

Mix bread and cornbread crumbs with onions, celery, parsley, apple, and seasonings. Add small amount of stock to moisten, then add melted butter and mix well. Add beaten eggs. Add enough stock to make a stuffing that holds together but is not wet or pasty. Yield: stuffing for 10-12-pound bird.

Table Grace

Some hae meat and canna eat,
And some wad eat that want it,
But we hae meat and we can eat
And so the Lord be thanket.

—The Selkirk Grace

Chapter 3   EARLY WINTER

December 2–January 10

DECEMBER is the month which the albatross chooses for laying its one egg of the year in the seas off the Cape of Good Hope. Apparently it finds these seas, during the middle two weeks of the month, calmer than at any other time of year. So, too, does this period seem to us a lull between the raging storms of November and the blizzards of winter. There is a breathing spell here with the weather as well as with ourselves for the adjustment of annual accounts—a year-end balancing which may bring, if the year has been a dry one, lots of rain, or if it has been on the cool side, a mild month.

In such a time as this, when the nights are twice as long

as our New England days, natives have often been heard to remark that if they can live through this shortest day of the year (December 21), then they will live a whole "nother" year, too!

"A green winter makes a full churchyard," is the old saying. And ancient books are filled with explanations as well as dire warnings connected with this old wives' tale. They say the earth—damp and cold and frozen as it is this time of year—gives off, especially at night, unhealthy vapors which, if the snow were upon the ground, would not be allowed to escape. Almost everybody likes to have an early snowfall that stays with us, not only as a blanket but also as a beautifier of the landscape. More fearsome, however, than a gray bare landscape is the heavy icestorm. Mark Twain considered such a storm "nature's most beautiful spectacle." But Mark Twain was a resident of the city of Hartford, Connecticut, when he said this in a speech before the New England Society of New York. Country folk can do without the beauties of such a storm. They hate to see their favorite trees bowed and often broken. And there is no great delight in driving on icy roads nor in trying to keep one's household perking without electricity.

Often, after such a storm, one wonders if nature is using a sort of control lest our trees become too large and cumbersome and greedy for the space allotted to their roots. For, like the hurricane or tornado which has somewhat similar results, there almost seems to be a necessary correcting force here which will literally cast to the ground branches that have become too long—and topple over trees whose roots are not strong enough to hold up trunk and branches, too.

These long wintry nights can offer a kind of beneficial relaxation many of us will not find at any other time of the year. We need such a period for the refilling of our spiritual wells by reading a favorite book again—or for dreaming before the colors and crackling of open fires. How often at other times of the year do we feel drowsy and tired though we keep going. Sleep seems such a waste of a good day or evening. But now, with the year's work nearly done, we can feel that nature almost expects us to relax and grow—like the trees—within.

On New Year's Day one has often heard it said, "The days have lengthened one cock's stride." This seems to have something to do with flat-stone farmhouse doorsteps which, if facing south, act as sundials on which a farmer's poultry might measure in their strides the difference in the position of shadows cast by a tree or rooftree. And by now at the end of "early winter," on January 10, no doubt we can say we are at least two cock's strides nearer spring and the first bluebird.

Winter is about to begin in earnest, however. The cold will be steady and we have had plenty of time to prepare our homes as well as ourselves for it. In fact, adjusted this way, and our bodies as well as our minds all a-tingle, we can turn to a full six weeks of healthy and progressive enjoyment—winter!

* * *

It is no single day that ushers in the winter season, but rather the dawning of an instinctive feeling that winter is

53

here and here to stay—until the dawning of a contrary feeling sometime in March. For most of us this means that a greater proportion of our time is spent indoors, and in some measure with the household arts.

This fits in nicely with the fact that the Christmas season is approaching, because we can go to work in the kitchen and make a lot of candies, fruit cake, and plum pudding for Christmas.

Pomander Balls

Select thin-skinned oranges, lemons, and limes. Pierce the skin at random to form an interesting pattern. Insert cloves. Roll oranges in cinnamon, covering with as thick a coating as possible. Roll lemons and limes in nutmeg. Wrap in foil and store for several weeks. Attach a sprig of holly at the top and bind with ribbon, with an extra loop for convenience in hanging the pomander ball as a decoration in the room or to give fragrance to your closet.

Dundee Cake

1 cup butter
1 cup sugar
5 eggs, beaten
1¼ cups flour
½ cup currants, diced
½ cup raisins
½ cup seedless grapes, diced
¼ cup whole almonds

½ cup candied orange peel, chopped
⅓ cup ground almonds
grated rind of 1 orange
⅛ teaspoon salt
¾ teaspoon soda
1 teaspoon milk

Cream butter and sugar. Add alternately beaten eggs and sifted flour. Beat well. Add fruit, ground almonds, grated rind, and

54

salt. Then add soda dissolved in milk. Turn into loaf pans lined with 2 layers of greased wrapping paper. Cover surface of cake with almonds. Bake in slow oven (300°) for 3 hours.

Yankee Christmas Pudding

14 slices bread	¼ teaspoon cloves
¼ pound citron, chopped	1½ cups sugar
¾ pound suet, chopped	1 teaspoon salt
2 cups currants	4 apples, chopped
2 cups raisins	¼ cup brandy
grated rind 1 lemon	6 eggs, beaten

Remove crusts from slightly stale bread. Crumb the bread and combine with the above ingredients. Place in two one-quart molds. Place molds in 1 inch boiling water in kettle. Cover kettle tightly and steam for 4 hours. Serve with hard sauce. Serves 12.

Plum Pudding

2 cups apples, chopped	1 cup molasses
1½ cups seedless raisins	1½ cups bread crumbs
1 cup nut meats	⅓ cup flour
½ cup candied orange peel	1 teaspoon cinnamon
1 cup cider	1 teaspoon cloves
1 cup suet, chopped	1 teaspoon allspice
½ cup brown sugar	1 teaspoon salt

3 eggs, well beaten

Combine apples, raisins, nuts, and orange peel with cider. Cover. Let stand 8 hours. Add suet, brown sugar, molasses, bread crumbs, flour, and seasonings. Stir in beaten eggs. Pour into buttered mold, filling two-thirds full. Place mold on trivet in kettle of boiling water (1 inch deep). Cover and steam 8 hours. Serve with sauce. Serves 12.

Governor Bradford's Plum Pudding

1 pound loaf of bread	1 cup seedless Sultana raisins
butter	1 cup seedless Muscatel raisins
3 cups boiling milk	1 cup currants
5 eggs, beaten	½ cup citron, shaved thin
1 cup dark molasses	½ cup candied cherries, halved
1 teaspoon salt	3 cups cold milk

Slice bread. Butter the slices and break into small pieces in a deep bowl. Cover with boiling milk and let bowl stand, closely covered, for 15 minutes. Mash bread with a fork, removing crusts that have not softened. Add eggs and molasses. Beat well. Add salt, raisins, currants, citron, cherries. Butter thickly a large pudding mold or bread pan. Pour in mixture, leaving 2 inches from top of pan. Set bread pan in a deep pan of hot water. Bake slowly for several hours. As crust forms on the pudding, gash with a knife and pour cold milk into the gash, one cupful at a time. When the knife comes out clean, the pudding is done. Leave pudding in mold until ready to serve. Serves 12.

Rum Sauce for Pudding

1 cup butter	5 tablespoons rum
3 cups confectioners' sugar	

Cream butter and sugar. Gradually add rum. Chill before serving.

Uncooked Fruit Cake

1½ cups dates	⅔ cup candied cherries
¾ cup raisins	1 cup candied pineapple
2 tablespoons orange juice	1½ cups walnuts or pecans
⅛ teaspoon salt	

Cut dates and raisins very fine. Combine in mixing bowl. Add orange juice. Cut up cherries, pineapple, and nut meats, and add to mixture. Add salt. Line pan with wax paper. Press mixture firmly into pan. Put weight on top and let stand in cold place for 48 hours. Yield: 1½ lbs. Keeps indefinitely.

Orange and Grapefruit Peel

2 grapefruit	2 cups sugar
4 oranges	¾ cup water
	ginger root

Peel the fruit, leaving white section on the peeling. Cut peelings into 2-inch strips. Cover with cold water, bring to a boil. Then discard water. Repeat this process five times. Drain carefully. Boil sugar and water until a thread forms from top of fork. Add peel and ginger root, and cook until the syrup thickens again. Drain peel and spread on wax paper. Roll in granulated sugar.

Honey Scotch

½ cup water	2 cups sugar
	½ cup honey

Heat water and sugar, stirring until sugar is dissolved. Add honey and cook, stirring gently to prevent scorching. Cook to hard crack stage (300°). Remove pan from heat and pour candy into buttered pan. When candy begins to set, cut into 1-inch-wide strips. Roll into cylinders. Cut with scissors into pieces 1 inch long. Yield: 1 pound.

Christmas Apples

6 apples   1 cup water
1½ cups sugar   ½ cup quince jelly
                    ¼ cup brandy

Select apples carefully. Pare and core, without disturbing the base of the apple. Make a syrup of sugar and water and simmer apples in it until tender but still firm. Place apples in serving dish. Fill center with jelly. Boil down the sugar syrup until quite thick, then pour over the apples. Pour brandy over the apples, light, and serve.

Horehound Candy

6 tablespoons horehound   1½ cups hot water
   leaves and stems   3½ cups brown sugar

Crush the herbs and place in teapot. Cover with very hot water and steep for about 30 minutes. Strain. Pour this liquid over brown sugar, mix, and bring to boil. Continue boiling until the liquid reaches hard crack stage (300°). Pour into buttered pan and cut into squares.

Molasses Popcorn Balls

3 quarts popped corn   ½ cup sugar
1½ cups molasses   2 teaspoons vinegar
¼ cup water   1 tablespoon vanilla
                    4 tablespoons butter

After corn is popped, discard imperfect kernels. Sprinkle corn with salt. Combine molasses, water, sugar, vinegar. Cook slowly, stirring constantly to hard ball stage. Remove from fire. Add vanilla flavoring and butter, stirring slightly. Pour over popcorn, stirring constantly. Grease hands and shape popcorn quickly into balls. Cool and wrap in wax paper. Makes 25 balls.

Angus Toffee

2 tablespoons butter	¼ cup ground almonds
3 cups sugar	1 cup milk

Melt butter in saucepan. Stir in sugar, almonds, and milk. Bring to a boil. Boil for 6 or 7 minutes, stirring constantly. When it begins to draw away from the sides of the pan (or reaches the hard crack stage, 300°), remove from the fire. Continue stirring until it is thick. Pour into buttered pan. When cool, cut with a sharp knife.

Old-Fashioned Butterscotch

2 cups brown sugar	½ cup butter
¼ cup molasses	2 tablespoons water
2 tablespoons vinegar	

Combine ingredients in deep saucepan. Bring to a boil quickly. Stir frequently, and when hard crack stage (300°) is reached, pour candy into buttered pan.

Angelica Candy

2 cups sugar	1 tablespoon lemon juice
2 cups water	1 pound angelica roots

Make syrup by boiling sugar and water for 30 minutes, adding lemon juice the last 5 minutes of cooking. Add angelica roots to the syrup and let stand until the mixture reaches room temperature. Then heat, bring to a boil. Boil for 30 minutes, until

59

syrup becomes candied. Drain off the syrup and put roots on wax paper until dry.

From December 1 on, anticipation, like a roll of drums, grows in intensity right up to Christmas dinner. Chicken or turkey will be the center of this feast for many, surrounded by mashed potatoes, turnips, squash, onions, sweet potatoes, watermelon preserve, sweet chopped piccalilli, mustard pickle, and, one hopes, a boat of dark brown gravy.

Since chicken is so often served the year round for Sunday dinner, many people like to serve, for Christmas, something unusual like pheasant, a suckling pig, or a green goose.

Roast Goose with Apples

1 10-pound goose, cleaned and drawn	½ onion, sliced
	6 peppercorns
4 cups water	¼ pound butter, melted

Wash goose inside and out. Drain. Cover with cold water and soak for 15 minutes. Drain, and pat dry. Rub well with salt inside and out. Place in baking pan. Add water, onion, and peppercorns. Roast in moderate oven (325°), allowing 20 minutes to the pound. Baste with butter frequently. Serves 6.

STEWED APPLES

6 apples	½ cup water
2 tablespoons butter	½ cup white wine
½ cup sugar	1 tablespoon lemon juice
	lemon peel

Peel apples and cut in thick slices. Sauté in butter for several minutes. Sprinkle with sugar. Add water, wine, lemon juice and peel. Cover and cook slowly until apples are tender. Serve with roast goose. Serves 6.

GOOSE DRESSING

12 potatoes, peeled and mashed	1 teaspoon goose fat or melted butter
2 onions, grated	1 teaspoon chopped parsley
1 egg, beaten	1 teaspoon thyme
salt and pepper	

Combine mashed potatoes, onions, egg, fat, and seasonings. Mix well. This dressing is sufficient for a 10- or 12-pound goose.

Crown Roast of Pork

Cover the tips of rib bones with small pieces of raw potato to prevent burning. Wrap bacon around the bones at the lower part of the crown. Rub the meat with salt, pepper, and flour. Fill the center with cranberry stuffing. Roast in a moderate oven (350°) 40 minutes to the pound. Replace potatoes with paper frills and serve.

Cranberry Stuffing

1½ cups cranberries	⅛ teaspoon pepper
4 tablespoons sugar	⅛ teaspoon thyme
⅓ cup melted butter	⅛ teaspoon dill
4 cups bread crumbs	1 tablespoon grated onion
1 teaspoon salt	1 garlic clove, mashed

Cut cranberries in very small pieces and mix with other ingredients. Cook over moderate heat for 10 minutes. Cool before using as a stuffing for the roast pork.

Old-fashioned Christmas dinners usually wound up with three kinds of pie—mince, pumpkin, and cranberry—and at various points of vantage, bowls of hickory nuts and walnuts with a nutcracker, as well as bowls of fruit and raisins and hard candy.

Parties now, as then, start well before Christmas Day, and continue right through New Year's eggnog. Every party must have its refreshments, usually punch for the children, and for the adults a wide variety of spirituous mixtures including hot buttered rum, rum punch, mead, syllabub, and Atholl Brose.

Mincemeat

4 pounds chopped beef
2 pounds chopped beef suet
6 quarts apples, peeled, cored, and chopped fine
2 pounds brown sugar
1 pound white sugar
1 pint cider
1 pint molasses
4½ pounds seeded raisins, finely chopped
2 pounds currants
1 pound chopped citron

½ pound finely chopped lemon peel, candied
½ pound finely chopped orange peel, candied
½ cup lemon juice
1 teaspoon pepper
1 teaspoon salt
1 gallon sour cherries and juice
1 pound nut meats
1 quart rum
1 tablespoon cinnamon
1 tablespoon cloves

2 whole grated nutmegs

Combine all ingredients except rum, cinnamon, cloves, and nutmeg. Simmer for 2 hours, then add remaining ingredients. Keep in a crock in cold room, or seal in jars.

Mincemeat Pie

Line pie pan with pie crust, fill with mincemeat. Cover with upper crust and bake in hot oven (450°) for 30 minutes.

Eggnog

6 eggs	1 pint bourbon
¾ cup sugar	1 ounce rum
1 pint whipping cream	1 pint milk

nutmeg

You will need three bowls. In the largest bowl beat the egg yolks until thick and lemon colored, add ½ cup sugar and stir until sugar is dissolved. In the second bowl beat the egg whites very stiff, but not dry, then add ¼ cup sugar. In the third bowl whip the cream until it stands in peaks. Begin by pouring a small quantity of bourbon over the yolks, stirring constantly, then add a small quantity of the egg whites and continue until all has been used; next stir in the whipped cream and more bourbon and rum; finally pour in the milk and stir gently. Chill for at least an hour before serving with a sprinkling of nutmeg. Yield: about 2 quarts.

This Harvard Club recipe can easily be scaled down to household size:

Eggnog

30 dozen eggs	12 pounds granulated sugar
30 bottles bourbon whisky	60 quarts heavy cream
5 bottles Jamaica rum	16 quarts milk

Separate eggs, using only yolks. Add whisky, rum, and sugar. Let stand for 3 hours. Stir in cream. Keep cool. Just before serving, add milk.

Coffee Punch

1 gallon coffee	16 teaspoons sugar
2 cups cream	2 quarts ice cream

Combine coffee, cream, and sugar. Pour over ice cream and serve in punch glasses. Serves 20.

Hot Buttered Rum

Dissolve 1 lump of sugar in a little hot water. Add a half pat of butter and a jigger (1 ounce) of rum. Fill glass with hot water. Sprinkle with nutmeg and cinnamon.

Christmas Rum Punch

6 oranges	sugar
cloves	8 cups sweet cider
1 pint rum	cinnamon
	nutmeg

Insert cloves in oranges. Heat in oven until they soften slightly. Place in punch bowl and pour rum over them. Add sugar to taste. Set fire to rum for a minute or two. Add cider very slowly, thus putting out the flame. Stir in cinnamon and nutmeg. Serve hot. Serves 12.

Mead

4 pounds brown sugar	4 ounces cream of tartar
½ pint molasses	1 ounce checkerberry
3 quarts boiling water	1 ounce sassafras

Mix brown sugar, molasses, and boiling water. Let stand. When lukewarm, add cream of tartar. When cold, add checkerberry and sassafras. Mix 2 tablespoons of this mixture in a glass of water with ⅓ teaspoon soda. Add ice. Serves 12.

Syllabub

3 ounces brandy	¼ pound powdered sugar
6 ounces white wine	2 cups cream
1 lemon	2 egg whites, beaten

Combine brandy and wine. Add lemon juice and rind, with sugar. Let stand overnight. Beat into this mixture the cream and egg whites. Serves 6.

Atholl Brose

4 sherry glasses oatmeal water	4 tablespoons honey
whisky to yield one quart	

Put oatmeal in bowl and mix with cold water until it forms a thick paste. Let stand for 30 minutes, then press through a strainer, leaving the meal as dry as possible. Discard meal, and use remaining liquid for the "brose." Blend honey and brose thoroughly. Put in a quart bottle and fill to the top with whisky. Shake well before serving. Keep tightly corked. Yield: 1 quart.

Chapter 4   WINTER

January 11–February 20

AUTHORITIES place the so-called "New England January Thaw" anywhere between the sixth and the thirtieth. Usually its arrival is during the last week of the month. A three-foot blanket of snow can disappear during this thaw almost overnight. Nor is there ever a January in which there is no thaw.

One remembers it from one's younger days more vividly than any blizzard. There was something fantastic about being able to go out in rubber boots, after weeks of freezing weather, to slosh around in rivers of open water. To launch an expedition on a wooden raft in the flooded meadow behind the house was really something. George Washington crossing the Delaware had nothing on us.

No one has ever offered any real explanation for this thaw, nor do there seem to be any superstitious sayings concerning it. It just comes as a warm "breather," sometimes welcome even if rainy, between cold spells or snowstorms.

In the few weeks before it, however, you may expect the coldest days of the year. There is no danger of thin or crumpling ice during these cold weeks except perhaps on rivers or lakes with bubbling springs. It is an ideal occasion to enjoy winter skating parties—morning, afternoon, or even in the full of an evening moon.

Or, perhaps, skiing. Those lucky enough to be in some small country town for the skiing probably won't do much thinking about what sort of place the town was before this sport became its winter livelihood. They won't picture, for example, teams of eight or ten horses—or sometimes even as many oxen—dragging a huge roller over snowy roads to make them suitable for sleighing as a simple, practical means of transportation.

Time was when at places like Woodstock, Vermont, skiers or snowshoers in a holiday mood set off in the morning from the village, packs on their backs, for extended cross-country tours. Noon would find them high above the village broiling steaks around a fire. Afternoon would find the skiers shooting down improvised trails or over the well-buried fences of broad white pastures. In those long-ago days, coasting with sleds or double runners on some hilly country roads was also a favorite sport.

Before you know it, Ground-hog Day, or Candlemas, has come and "winter is half over." On this day, February 2, the frost is as deep in the ground as it will be this winter, and possibly has awakened Mr. and Mrs. Ground Hog. They will come up to the surface and see how things are. The ancient superstition is that if the sun is out and they see their shadows, they will scamper down into their hole again and sleep another six weeks. If, however, it is a cloudy day and no shadows are visible, then they will know winter is about over and an early spring is near at hand.

We are at midpoint on this day in the coldest forty days of the year. The sun is noticeably higher now, and some of the earliest flowering shrubs like the hobblebush can be broken off and brought into the house to flower. Of even more importance is this warmth of the February sun to the window-box garden.

Breeders of poultry, especially, will be careful to note this slow approach of the sun to the spring solstice. A neighboring farmer goes a lot by this in the planning of his hatching and raising. The native African wild jungle fowl is the bird from which all varieties of poultry are derived. This native jungle fowl still makes a point of hatching her spring broods on the exact day of the solstice. The neighboring farmer tells us that chicks hatched on this day in New England will do better and lay earlier than chicks hatched at any other time.

It is the beginning—here in early February—of the growing season. As clues to this change, there is much in nature to observe. If one lives near a waterfall, it is interesting to follow ice formations on the bed of the brook under the water. Sometimes the ice will let go, rise, and be swept downstream—a sure sign of warmer weather, perhaps even rain. Why? Because the cold will be starting to come up out of the earth now and into the atmosphere. In this process, it will free the ice.

But there is nothing more beautiful in all the year than February's early mornings. Not too early—just when the sun, after heavy frosts or the night's cold, comes to greet the many crystals on the surface of the snow fields. How crisp, how glistening, how invigorating the warming air, and how filled with exciting hopes for this very day about to come!

On the third Thursday of February, you may be celebrating the Fair of Auld St. Deer—noted as the day of the year's worst weather. It has this reputation because for centuries in Scotland an important cattle fair has been held on this day. Invariably, we are told, it will rain, snow, sleet, and blow for that occasion. So, too, in New England, in almost any year, you will find a first-class blizzard showing up about this time—1717, 1843, 1899, 1921, and 1956, to name just a few.

Blizzards can be fun. You can tell one by the way the snow blows off the flat roof over the porch where the latter makes an angle with the house. There is a sweep and swush to it as fascinating to watch as any wild breaker on a beach. It is a time when the town snow-clearing equipment will be overtaxed—a good time to stay home and not care whether one is snowed in for a while or not.

Until 1582, when the calendar was changed, February was the last month of the year, as it normally is the end of winter. With but a few weeks of winter remaining, it will be well to take a long last look. Held firmly in its frozen grip, we can wriggle a bit, and perhaps escape momentarily from its gray and somber clutches into the fascination of some of its beauties. There are, for example, these snow crystals. Find an unheated room on one of these very cold mornings—one in which the windows face the morning sun—and note the silhouettes of forests, lakes, and mountains painted on the glass. You will see millions of tiny crystals—all six-sided—and each crystal different from any other on the pane, or for that matter on any other pane anywhere.

Given a lifetime project of making different designs of three- or six-sided forms, how quickly would one run out of ideas. Yet nature somehow manages not only a complete and magnificent difference in each of these separate crystal "cells," but also paints an endless variety of scenes and subjects with them—each of these different, too.

Now, too, before the snows have melted and gone away, a winter walk in the woods on snowshoes, skis, or even on foot is something you will not soon forget. Especially interesting are the tracks in the snow of winter animals still about—the porcupine, fox, partridge, pheasant, cat, squirrel, titmouse, deer, and rabbit. You may have heard about conclaves of rabbits in the full of the February moon, and perhaps seen tracks in the woods indicating something of the sort had happened.

* * *

Wrapped tightly in the chilly embrace of winter, we cast about for ways to steer our food on a new and interesting tack.

What could possibly taste better to those coming in out of

the cold than a thick slice of hot homemade bread sloshy with melted butter? Get out the mixing bowl and heat up the oven!

White Bread

1 cup scalded milk	2½ tablespoons sugar
1 cup boiling water	2 teaspoons salt
1 tablespoon lard	1 yeast cake
1 tablespoon butter	¼ cup warm water

6 to 8 cups flour

Combine scalded milk and boiling water, and pour into large mixing bowl containing lard, butter, sugar, and salt. Let stand until lukewarm. Then add yeast cake dissolved in warm water. Sift flour and gradually add to the mixture. The dough should remain moist and sticky. Knead on floured board until smooth and elastic. Place dough in greased bowl, cover, and let rise in a warm place until it doubles in bulk (about 4 hours). Knead, adding more flour if necessary, shape into loaves, and place in two greased bread pans (5 x 10 inches), filling half-full. Cover and let rise until it doubles in bulk. Bake in hot oven (450°) for 10 minutes. Then reduce to moderate oven (350°) and bake 30 minutes longer. Makes two loaves.

Anadama Bread

½ cup yellow corn meal	2½ teaspoons salt
2 cups boiling water	2 cakes yeast
2 tablespoons shortening	½ cup warm water
½ cup molasses	7 cups flour

Add corn meal gradually to boiling water, stirring constantly. Add shortening, molasses, and salt. Let stand until lukewarm.

Dissolve yeast cakes in warm water and add to corn-meal mixture. Sift flour and stir in well so that the dough is smooth and rather thick. Knead well. Place in greased bowl, cover, and let rise in warm place until it doubles in bulk. Cut through the dough several times with a knife, cover, and let rise again for about 40 minutes. Knead on floured board, adding more flour if necessary. Form into two loaves and place in greased loaf pans. Cover, and let rise until it doubles in bulk. Bake in hot oven (450°) for 15 minutes, then reduce heat to moderate oven (350°) and bake 45 minutes longer. Brush with melted fat. Makes two loaves.

Crackling Bread

1½ cups corn meal   3 tablespoons sugar
¾ cup flour   1 cup sour milk
1 teaspoon baking powder   1¼ cups salt pork cracklings

Mix and sift corn meal, flour, baking powder, and sugar. Add milk. Dice cracklings and stir into the mixture. Turn into muffin tins, or cake pans. Bake in hot oven (400°) for 30 minutes. Yield: about 16 muffins.

Parker House Rolls

1 cup scalded milk   1 teaspoon salt
1 tablespoon sugar   ½ yeast cake
2 tablespoons butter   ¼ cup warm water
                3 cups flour

Add sugar, butter, and salt to scalded milk. Let stand until lukewarm, then add yeast cake dissolved in warm water. Sift flour and add to mixture until it is stiff enough to knead. Knead, and place in greased bowl. Cover and let rise in warm place until it doubles in bulk, about 2 hours. Shape the dough into balls, and with the floured handle of a wooden spoon, press the balls through the center. Brush one half with butter, and fold the other half over, pressing lightly. Let rise again in warm place, about 40 minutes. Bake in hot oven (425°) for about 15 minutes. Brush tops with butter. Yield: 2 dozen rolls.

These rolls were originated by Harvey D. Parker, founder of the hotel that bears his name.

Rhode Island Johnnycake

1 cup Rhode Island white johnnycake corn meal (preferably waterground)	1 teaspoon salt
	1 teaspoon sugar
	1¼ cups boiling water

Mix corn meal, salt, and sugar. Add water gradually to form a rather thick batter. Bake on greased skillet. Cake should be about ⅛-inch thick and well cooked before turning. Cook to golden brown. Serve with butter. Yield: 1 dozen.

Walnut Brown Bread

2 cups graham flour	2 cups sweet milk
1½ cups white flour	1 teaspoon salt
½ cup brown sugar	1½ teaspoons soda
½ cup molasses	1 cup chopped walnuts, fine

Beat light. Bake in one loaf one hour.

—from an old cook book—

Raisin Bread

½ cup butter
½ cup sugar
1½ cups raisins
1 tablespoon salt

1½ cups milk
2 yeast cakes
⅓ cup warm water
4 eggs, beaten

5 cups sifted flour

Combine butter, sugar, raisins, and salt. Heat milk and pour over it. Cool. Dissolve yeast cakes in warm water. Add to milk mixture. Then add beaten eggs. Mix in 5 cups flour, adding more flour if necessary. Stir well. Let rise until double in bulk. Knead. Let rise again. Put into two buttered bread pans. Brush top with butter and sprinkle with sugar. Let rise again. Bake in moderate oven (375°) for 50 minutes.

A cake-making spree is another way to sweeten the bitter winter. You're sure to make chocolate cake to please the men just as Yankee women did way back when they lived in a British colony. They made such cakes to celebrate the return of a sailing ship from the East with a cargo of cocoa beans aboard. So slim was the supply, and so high the cost, that the ingenious housewives worked out a way to make the chocolate go twice as far, inventing marble cake.

Even before the Revolution, this shortage was being corrected through the partnership of Dr. James Baker of Dorchester, Massachusetts, and John Hannon, an Irish immigrant. They established the chocolate mill that later became Walter Baker and Company. Baker's Breakfast Cocoa and German's Sweet Chocolate, developed ninety years later by an English immigrant, Samuel German, have been favorites for eating, cake, pudding, and pie-making ever since.

Even with chocolate plentiful, the marble cake has never lost its popularity.

Black and Gold Marble Cake

2 squares unsweetened
    chocolate, melted
3 tablespoons hot water
¼ teaspoon soda
2 tablespoons sugar
2½ cups sifted cake flour
1½ teaspoons baking powder

½ teaspoon soda
1 teaspoon salt
1⅔ cups sugar
¾ cup butter
¾ cup buttermilk or sour
    milk
1 teaspoon vanilla

3 eggs, unbeaten

Combine melted chocolate, hot water, ¼ teaspoon soda, and 2 tablespoons sugar. Set aside. Measure sifted flour into sifter. Add baking powder, ½ teaspoon soda, salt, and sugar. Let butter stand so that it will be room temperature. Sift in dry ingredients. Add buttermilk and vanilla, and mix until all flour is dampened. Beat for about 3 minutes. Then add eggs and beat 1½ minutes. Line two round 9-inch layer pans with paper. Put large spoonfuls of the plain and chocolate batters into pans, alternating the mixtures. Then with a knife cut through the first batter in a wide zigzag course to give marble effect. Bake in moderate oven (350°) 35 minutes.

Chocolate Dream Frosting

1 3-ounce package cream
    cheese
¼ cup milk

dash of salt
4 cups confectioners'
    sugar

3 squares unsweetened chocolate, melted

Soften cream cheese with part of milk. Add salt. Then add sugar, alternating with milk, blending well after each addition. Add chocolate and beat until smooth and of right consistency to spread. Yield: 2 cups.

Peppermint Boiled Frosting

1⅓ cups sugar
⅛ teaspoon salt
½ teaspoon light corn syrup
⅓ cup hot water

3 egg whites
¼ cup crushed hard
    peppermint candy
red coloring

Combine sugar, salt, corn syrup, and water. Bring quickly to a boil, stirring only until sugar is dissolved. Boil rapidly, without stirring, to soft ball stage. Beat egg whites until peaks form. Pour syrup over egg whites, beating constantly. Continue beating 10 to 15 minutes, or until frosting is cool and of right consistency to spread. Fold in peppermint candy. Sprinkle a small amount of coarsely crushed candy over top of frosted cake. Yield: 2 cups.

Chocolate Mint Cake

2¼ cups sifted cake flour
1 teaspoon soda
1 teaspoon salt
1¼ cups sugar
½ cup cocoa
½ cup sugar

½ cup sour milk or
    buttermilk
½ cup vegetable shortening
1 cup sour milk or buttermilk
1 teaspoon vanilla
2 eggs, unbeaten

Measure sifted flour into sifter. Add soda, salt, and 1¼ cups sugar. Combine cocoa, ½ cup sugar, and ½ cup milk. Set aside. Stir shortening just to soften. Sift in dry ingredients. Add 1 cup milk and vanilla, and mix until all flour is dampened. Beat about 3 minutes. Then add eggs and cocoa mixture, and beat for about 1½ minutes. Pour batter into two round 9-inch layer pans, lined with paper. Bake in moderate oven (350°) for 30 minutes.

Wellesley Fudge Cake

⅔ cup butter	⅔ cup boiling water
2⅔ cups brown sugar	2⅔ cups flour
1 egg	1½ teaspoons baking powder
3 egg yolks	pinch of salt
4 ounces unsweetened chocolate	⅔ cup sour milk
	1¼ teaspoons soda, dissolved

1 teaspoon vanilla

Cream butter and sugar. Add egg, then egg yolks, beating well after each addition. Make paste in double boiler of chocolate and boiling water. Add to butter-sugar-egg mixture. Sift flour three times before measuring. Then sift with baking powder and salt. Combine the mixtures, alternating with sour milk and soda. Add vanilla. Bake in moderate oven (350°) in two 9-inch square pans.

Wellesley Fudge Cake Frosting

4 squares unsweetened chocolate	2 tablespoons butter
powdered sugar	1 teaspoon vanilla
	½ cup chopped walnuts

Melt chocolate in double boiler. Add powdered sugar to give consistency to spread. Add butter, then vanilla. Cool slightly. Spread between layers and on top of cake. Sprinkle with nut meats.

Black Walnut Cake

½ cup butter	2 cups sifted flour
1¼ cups powdered sugar	2½ teaspoons baking powder
½ cup milk	1 cup coarsely chopped black walnut meats
1 teaspoon vanilla	

4 egg whites

Cream butter and sugar. Beat in milk and vanilla. Add sifted

77

flour and baking powder, then add nut meats. Fold in stiffly beaten egg whites. Bake in buttered 9 x 13-inch pan in moderate oven (350°) for 25-30 minutes.

Scripture Cake

1 cup butter	Judges 5:25
3½ cups flour	I Kings 4:22
2 cups sugar	Jer. 6:20
2 cups raisins	I Sam. 30:12
2 cups figs	I Sam. 30:12
1 cup water	Gen. 24:17
1 cup almonds	Gen. 43:11
6 eggs	Isa. 10:14
1 tablespoon honey	Exod. 16:21
a pinch of salt	Lev. 2:13
spices to taste	I Kings 10:10
½ teaspoon soda	Matt. 13:33
1 teaspoon cream tartar	Matt. 13:33
Father Solomon's advice for making good boys	Prov. 23:13

—from an old cook book—

Election Cake

2 cups milk, scalded
½ cup brown sugar, tightly
    packed
½ teaspoon salt
1 yeast cake
5 cups flour, sifted
1½ cups sugar

¾ cup shortening
2 eggs
1½ cups raisins
¼ pound citron, sliced thin
    (optional)
½ teaspoon nutmeg
½ teaspoon mace

Place milk, brown sugar, and salt in mixing bowl. When luke-warm, add crumbled yeast cake and 4½ cups of the flour. Beat thoroughly and let rise overnight. In the morning, cream sugar and shortening, and add to mixture. Stir in eggs, raisins, citron, nutmeg, mace, and remaining flour. Mix thoroughly. Place in greased bread tins, lined with wax paper, also greased. Let rise until double in bulk. Bake in moderate hot oven (375°) about 50 minutes. Makes 2 loaves.

Molasses came back to New England on the first Yankee sailing ships to trade with the West Indies. Quickly, the men found out how to make it into rum, and the women used it to create new recipes that since have become traditional.

Old-Fashioned Molasses Cookies

½ cup butter	½ cup sour milk
½ cup brown sugar	2½ cups flour
1 egg	½ teaspoon ginger
1 cup molasses	½ teaspoon nutmeg
1 teaspoon baking soda	1 teaspoon cinnamon

1 teaspoon salt

Cream butter and sugar. Beat egg and add to mixture. Then add molasses, soda, and sour milk. Beat well. Sift flour and seasonings; add to mixture. Blend well. Drop onto greased baking pan. Bake 10-12 minutes in moderate oven (375°). Yield: about 40 cookies.

Molasses Pie

3 eggs	¼ cup melted butter
1 cup brown sugar	1 cup pecans
1 cup molasses	1 teaspoon vanilla
⅓ teaspoon salt	1 9-inch pie crust

Line 9-inch pan with pie crust. Beat eggs, sugar, molasses, salt, and butter until sugar is dissolved and mixture has sirupy consistency. Add pecans and vanilla. Pour into pie crust. Bake in moderate oven (375°) for 45-50 minutes.

Baked Indian Pudding

5 cups milk	¾ teaspoon cinnamon
⅔ cup dark molasses	¼ teaspoon nutmeg
⅓ cup sugar	½ teaspoon salt
½ cup yellow corn meal	2 tablespoons butter

Scald 3 cups of the milk. Add molasses, sugar, corn meal, spices, salt, and butter. Cook 20 minutes, or until mixture thickens. Pour into buttered baking dish. Add remaining 2 cups milk. Do not stir. Bake 3 hours in slow oven (300°). Serve warm with cream. Serves 8.

Gingerbread I

1½ cups flour	1½ cups molasses
¼ teaspoon salt	½ cup candied lemon peel,
½ cup oatmeal	shredded
1 cup butter	2 tablespoons ginger
½ cup cream	

Mix flour, salt, and oatmeal. Cream butter. Add flour mixture and cream alternately. Stir in molasses, lemon peel, and ginger.

80

Work into a light dough, turn into a well-greased pan. Bake in moderate oven (350°) for 40 minutes.

Gingerbread II

1 cup flour	¼ teaspoon salt
1 teaspoon baking soda	½ cup raisins, seedless
1 teaspoon cinnamon	¼ cup almonds, blanched
1 teaspoon cloves	½ cup butter
1 teaspoon nutmeg	4 tablespoons sugar
1½ teaspoons ginger	½ cup molasses

2 eggs, beaten

Sift flour, soda, spices, and salt. Add diced raisins and almonds. Bring butter, sugar, and molasses to a boil, and pour over beaten eggs. Stir well. Combine this mixture with dry ingredients. Beat well. Put into buttered cake pan. Bake in moderate oven (350°) for one hour.

Maine Molasses Doughnuts

2 eggs	4 cups flour
1 cup sugar	¼ teaspoon cloves
½ cup molasses	¼ teaspoon ginger
1 cup sour milk	⅛ teaspoon salt
1 teaspoon soda	1 tablespoon melted lard

Beat eggs, add sugar, and beat well. Add molasses, sour milk, and soda. Sift flour with spices and salt, and add to mixture. Then add melted shortening. Roll out a few doughnuts at a time and fry in deep hot fat. Turn frequently; drain. Yield: 3 dozen.

Boston Cream Pie

CAKE

2 cups cake flour, sifted	1 cup sugar
3 teaspoons baking powder	1 egg
¼ teaspoon salt	¾ cup milk
4 tablespoons butter	1 teaspoon vanilla

Sift together flour, baking powder, and salt. Resift twice again. Cream butter and sugar. Add unbeaten egg and beat well. Add flour mixture alternately with mix, beating after each addition. Add vanilla. Bake in two well-greased 8-inch layer pans in moderate oven (350°) about 25 minutes.

CREAM FILLING

½ cup sugar	2 eggs, beaten
½ cup flour	2 cups scalded milk
¼ teaspoon salt	1 teaspoon vanilla
	1 tablespoon butter

Combine sugar, flour, and salt. Mix with eggs. Stir in hot milk. Cook over boiling water for 10 minutes, stirring constantly. Cool. Add vanilla. Then add butter. Spread cream filling between the cake layers. Dust with powdered sugar on top.

Pound Cake

2 cups butter	4 cups cake flour
2 cups sugar	(sift before measuring)
2 tablespoons rosewater	10 eggs

Cream butter and sugar. Gradually add rosewater and one cup of flour. Whisk eggs until very thick. Stir in butter and sugar gradually, then the remainder of flour, a small quantity at a time. Beat well. Pour into pan lined with wax paper. Bake in moderate (350°) oven one hour.

At this time of year, the tackle of most fishermen is safely stored away, but not that of the most ardent fisherman of all, the ice fisherman. He gets out his spud, skimmer, bucket, and tilts, turns his back on the cozy hearth, and heads for the harsh bitterness of a winter-swept pond. This man's family can count itself luckiest of all, because, more often than not, he'll bring home fish from the icy water—calling for just a little culinary sleight-of-hand.

Perch, pike, pickerel, and catfish will probably be the ones found under the ice. The small pike may be pan-fried, and the larger fish broiled or stuffed and baked. Pickerel, too, may be fried, broiled, or baked, according to their size. Catfish are usually fried.

Baked Fish with Sour Cream

Split and remove bones from fish. Rub inside and out with butter and paprika. Place under flame until lightly browned. Then cover with sour cream. Cover the pan and bake in moderate oven (325°) for about 40 minutes.

Baked Fish with Almond Sauce

Roll fish fillets in seasoned bread crumbs. Let stand for half an hour to dry. Brown the fish in melted butter, then bake until done. Serve with ½ cup blanched almonds sautéed in 6 tablespoons butter. Season to taste.

Another attack upon the monotony with which our meals are threatened in the winter can be made by cultivating herbs in window boxes and sparking up our daily dishes with these home-grown greens. Many herbs can be grown successfully indoors. A little pinch of home-grown herbs has transformed many a dish from the commonplace to the exciting.

The following herbs are best suited for window boxes and the New England climate:

lemon balm	horehound	rue
wild bergamot	hyssop	sage
burnet	leek	sorrel
camomile	lovage	tansy
caraway	marjoram	tarragon
catnip	mint	thyme
chives	orégano	lemon verbena
fennel	rosemary	woodruff

Canapés

Combine cream cheese or cottage cheese with one of the following:

caraway	parsley
chives	rue
sage	

Eggs

Breakfast and Sunday omelettes will taste different each time you serve them—

basil	dill
chervil	parsley
chives	rosemary
savory	

Herb Teas

Prepare tea in the usual way, using the herb leaves instead of tea leaves. Steep 3 to 4 minutes.

lemon balm	fennel	mint
burnet	horehound	rosemary
camomile	hyssop	sage
caraway	love	thyme
catnip	marjoram	lemon verbena
	woodruff	

Herb Butter

Allow butter (sweet) to soften at room temperature. Place layer of fresh herb leaves in bottom of jar (with tight-fitting top); place butter in jar; add a top layer of herbs. Cover and let stand at room temperature for an hour. Refrigerate. Remove herbs when served.

caraway	rosemary
chives	sage
mint	tarragon
orégano	thyme

Vegetables and Herbs

Beans: with thyme
Beets: with thyme or chervil
Cabbage: with savory or tarragon or sorrel
Carrots: with thyme or mint
Eggplant: with basil or chervil
Onions: with sage or thyme
Cauliflower: with caraway
Potatoes: with caraway or thyme or rue or mint
Peas: with mint or sage

Game and Herbs

When cooking duck and pheasant, use hyssop. With venison, try marigold or rosemary. And use rosemary with partridge, rabbit, pheasant, duck, and quail.

Salads and Herbs

Mix with garden greens any of the following:

chives	lovage
fennel	sorrel
hyssop	tarragon
leek	water cress

Meat and Herbs

Mint with lamb, of course. But try orégano, too.
Rosemary with roast beef or pork, and also in veal.
Chives almost everywhere—with liver—add just before serving.
Sage with pork and veal.
Marjoram with chopped meats, lamb, and pork.
Tarragon with chicken; thyme in stews and fricassees.
And parsley, of course, with everything.

Fish and Herbs

Before *baking* fish, add one of these herbs:

marjoram	savory
orégano	tansy
sage	tarragon

thyme

Before *broiling* fish, add one of these:

marjoram	savory
rosemary	tarragon
thyme	

Use as *garnish* and for added flavor:

fennel	mint
hyssop	parsley

Recipe for a Clear Complexion

Peel and slice a horse-radish. Boil in rich milk, adding a few grams of sublimated sulphur. Boil for about 10 minutes, then put through a sieve. Put into bottle. Crush a handful of green leeks, boil the juice in milk. Put through a sieve. Bottle. Twice a week, wash the face with a combination of the two liquids (half of each), and notice the gradual change in complexion.

AROMATIC BATH

Boil the following herbs in a bag for 30 minutes in six quarts of water: lavender, mint, thyme, sage, rosemary, marjoram, wormwood, fennel. Add this water to bath water. Do not remain more than 30 minutes in this bath.

—from an old cook book—

Chapter 5   EARLY SPRING

February 21–April 1

AFTER Washington's Birthday there will still be a full allotment of storms, blizzards, rains, and floods. Until well into April the period must certainly be known as weeks of many weathers. It is an exciting time, however— one we would not exchange for any other. For in these forty days the year is born again.

It begins in the pink buds of the maples. Some think the March full moon is the instigator of it all for, as it rises, the pulse or rhythm of sap running in the maples quickens its beat. Others see a creative chemistry in the combination of cold nights and warm sunny days. For whatever reason, after many months of inactivity, now, before spring is really apparent, the sap in the roots of the maple trees begins its resistless upward coursing to trunk and limb, branch and leaf.

The native American Indians knew of this long before any white men came to these lands. They collected the sap of the sugar maples, in watertight baskets, and boiled it by tossing in heated stones. Today, a sugar orchard—as their maple trees are called—makes a valuable off-season occupation as well as income for many farmers in the northeastern part of the country.

There is a good deal of romance in it, too: the hanging of the buckets, the gathering of the run, the readying of fires in the sap house, and the boiling down of the syrup. Depending upon the kind of winter, snow may still be waist deep around the trees—or, after heavy rains and thaws, there may be none at all.

Some farmers sell their entire output of syrup to business firms to give away as presents to their customers. Others sell to converters who combine the pure maple syrup with sugar cane syrup and resell it at a lower price than is possible with the pure maple syrup. Sometimes it is put into candy boxes as maple sugar hearts or various other shapes for gift-shop sale. Happy people those who buy the real thing at this time of year! Maple syrup, freshly made, beats sulphur and molasses as a spring tonic all hollow. Dipped from the boiling pan, still hot, though not too hot to drink, it seems to course through the veins even as the sap itself is doing in the trees.

We do not know exactly what the chemical ingredients of maple syrup are. It does not say on the can, and we are not sure we really care. But at no other time do we crave this tonic as we do at the beginning of nature's new year. Its very sweetness seems to smooth away all of winter's rough edges. It relaxes us, too, so that we may enjoy the warm March sun, yet fortifies us strangely against the colds and snows we may still endure.

You may see a crocus or two around now and some of the earlier flowering shrubs, like the forsythia—or even fruit tree branches—can be brought into the house to bloom.

Of far greater import will be the beginning of Lent and its forty days to Easter. With the fasting and abnegation that go with the cleansing of the spirit during this holy time, the ancients observed many curious customs.

For instance, the Monday preceding Shrove Tuesday, or Mardi Gras, was known as Collop Monday. Slices of meat taken from carcasses hung up for the winter—for instance, slices of bacon or ham—were known as collops. It is supposed that, with Lent so near at hand, feasts featuring a large proportion of these meats helped use up the supply which the fasts of Lent would only leave to rot.

From the ancient Greek church derives the custom of eating pancakes on Mardi Gras. Here on this day before Ash Wednesday—the beginning of Lent—milk, eggs, cheese, and pancakes seem to have been the rule. One often hears the day actually called Pancake Tuesday. This particular Tuesday has been noted for hundreds of years also as a day by which to tell the weather.

"Some say thunder on Shrove Tuesday foretelleth wind, store of fruit, and plenty. Others affirm that so much as the sun shineth that day, the like will shine every day in Lent."

There is a nice coincidence anyhow when "Glad Shrove Tuesday brings the pancake thin/Or fritter rich, with apples stored within," because often maple syrup and Shrove Tuesday arrive on the scene at just about the same time.

The word Lent in the Saxon language signified spring. It originally began with what is now counted the first Sunday in Lent and ended on Easter Eve. However, that made forty-two days, and if the six Sundays on which in olden times it was unlawful to fast were subtracted, that left thirty-six. Consequently, Pope Gregory added to Lent the four days of the week before the first Sunday; namely, that day which we now call Ash Wednesday and the three days following it.

As Ash Wednesday is determined each year by the full of the moon nearest to the spring equinox (usually March 21), Lent itself is as slithery, calendarwise, as the season for which it is named.

Mid-Lent Sunday, the fourth Sunday in Lent, is a time when most of the small hibernating animals are coming out of their winter holes and hiding places. The chipmunks, raccoons, woodchucks, and skunks—many times with recently born young—come to the strong March sun to join some of the early birds and a landscape now fast coming to a new life again.

How long, we wonder, has this winter of sleep in the stillness of their underground rooms and passageways seemed to them? Nothing there has served—as surface signs would have—to remind them of night or day, of the passing of weeks and even months. Depending upon how deep in the ground their abode, only a fractional daily difference in temperature may have been noted. Humans could scarcely imagine how still the silence these little animals have known for many weeks. Now even the bursting of the buds and the opening of leaves must seem to them as cannon shots would to us.

A lovely superstition about Easter Day says the sun always dances on this day. This can be seen by placing a large glass dish full of water in the open air. The reflected sun will seem to dance. Or near a pond, lake, or the sea, you can see the sunlight quivering or tossing about on the surface. Perhaps it is just the angle the earth is making with the sun, but it is not too much to ask of even this unpoetic age that, feeling joyful on this great day, we should think it almost a disparagement of the Saviour if the sun did not join us in sympathetic exultation.

One of nature's best displays is her March clouds. With the trees not yet leafed out, this is a favorite time for us to seek a well-warmed rock along a wood path and sprawl back on it to observe these clouds. They will almost always be on the go—racing across the heavens—in marvelous white billowy shapes and forms. Through the designs of the lacy forest overhead, none will remain framed for long.

They remind us that the real cold weather is almost gone. There will be more snows perhaps and some shoveling, but we have already met the winter's challenge and have won. This is a glorious and expansive feeling—winter gone, but spring chores not yet upon us. Here in these few weeks— almost too few—we can relax before the rush of spring and summer is upon us. Even the mud season has not arrived.

To carry this opening up of nature, her billowing white clouds, blue sky, and promise of what is to come, into the house is something we all would like to do, but do not know quite how. Yes, a few bulbs are coming along and one or two of the storm windows can be taken off, though it is too early for most spring vegetables and greens.

Somewhere along in here comes April Fool's Day. It has a much longer and more interesting history than most people suppose. Actually such a day has been marked for centuries, perhaps beginning with the Romans, as a day of celebration. It is the time of the spring equinox—the sun is entering the sign of Aries, the New Year, and with it comes the season of vernal sport and rural delight. As for the connection between the day and the foolery, we can perhaps accept the humorous Jewish origin. This is said to have begun from the mistake Noah made in sending the dove out of the ark before the waters had abated on the first day of the month, which corresponds among the Hebrews to our first of April. To perpetuate the memory of this deliverance, whosoever forgot so remarkable a circumstance was sent forth on some fool's errand to remind him or her of it.

* * *

During the hurly-burliest season of all—which makes promises of spring one day and breaks them the next—our food has similar ups and downs from the joy of maple syrup to the deprivation of Lent, to the feast on Easter Sunday.

There is no set date for the maple sap to start running; we only know that the pulse of the trees' circulation flutters and buckets appear in every sugar orchard in New England. The pattern is simple: from a thousand trees, to the sugar

93

house, to a thousand kitchens. And in the thousand kitchens
maple syrup will undoubtedly be served with pancakes.

Vermont Thins

1 cup flour, sifted	2 tablespoons maple syrup
1½ teaspoons baking powder	1 egg, beaten
¼ teaspoon salt	1 cup milk

3 tablespoons melted shortening

Sift flour, baking powder, and salt. Combine maple syrup, egg,
and milk, and add gradually to flour mixture. Then add shortening. Cook on very hot greased griddle. Serves 4.

Potato Pancakes

2 cups potatoes, grated	1½ tablespoons flour
2 eggs, beaten	¼ teaspoon baking powder

1 teaspoon salt

Peel potatoes and grate into bowl of water. Squeeze dry. Combine with eggs, then add dry ingredients. Sauté in hot fat. Serve
with applesauce. Serves 4.

Blueberry Pancakes

¾ cup flour	2 eggs, beaten
½ teaspoon salt	1 cup milk
1 teaspoon baking powder	½ teaspoon vanilla
2 tablespoons powdered	1½ tablespoons butter
sugar	1 cup blueberries

powdered sugar

Sift dry ingredients, then add beaten eggs and liquid ingredients.
Combine with a few quick strokes. Melt butter, when hot pour

94

into pan one half the batter for each pancake. Fill with blueberries, then pour remaining half of batter over the fruit. Brown both sides. Serve hot with powdered sugar. Serves 4.

Elderberry Blossom Fritters

Wash the elderberry flowers, including the stem. Dry. Dip in batter recipe given above and fry.

Buckwheat Cakes

1 yeast cake	4 cups buckwheat flour
¼ cup warm water	2 cups water
1 teaspoon sugar	1 teaspoon salt

Dissolve yeast cake in warm water. Add sugar. Make a stiff batter of flour, water, and salt. Add yeast. Let rise. Let batter stand overnight in a warm place, for use at breakfast. Serve with maple syrup. Serves 4.

Each day save a small amount of the batter for use in making the next batch of griddle cakes. As the batter grows older, use a little white flour in the mixings, and also a little soda. After a few mixings, discard the old batter and begin anew.

Maple Syrup Pie

1½ tablespoons butter	1½ cups maple syrup
2 tablespoons flour	1 cup chopped walnuts
2 egg yolks	½ teaspoon vanilla
⅛ teaspoon salt	1 8-inch baked pie shell
	whipped cream

Cream butter and flour. Add egg yolks, salt, maple syrup. Cook in double boiler until thick. Add nut meats and vanilla. Pour into baked pie shell. Top with whipped cream.

Eggs in Maple Syrup

3 tablespoons maple sugar	3 eggs
¼ cup water	¼ teaspoon salt

Melt maple sugar in water, gradually bring to a boil. Beat eggs with salt and whip into maple mixture. Serve immediately on toast. Serves 2.

Pecan Pie

3 eggs	⅓ teaspoon salt
1 cup brown sugar	1 cup pecan halves
1 cup maple syrup	1 teaspoon vanilla
¼ cup melted butter	1 9-inch pie shell

Beat eggs, sugar, maple syrup, butter, and salt until sugar is dissolved. Blend in pecans. Add vanilla. Pour into pie shell. Bake in moderate oven (375°) for 50 minutes. Serve warm.

Maple Raisin Pudding

3 cups milk	1 teaspoon salt
⅔ cup maple syrup	6 slices bread, buttered
2 whole eggs, beaten	½ cup raisins
2 egg yolks, beaten	1 teaspoon cinnamon

Bring milk and maple syrup to a boil, then pour over the eggs, beating constantly. Add salt. Line oven-proof dish with pieces of buttered bread, sprinkle raisins over bread, and pour custard mixture over it. Sprinkle with cinnamon. Bake 45 minutes in moderate oven (350°). Serves 6.

Maple Sauce

2 cups maple syrup	½ cup nut meats, chopped

Boil the syrup for about 5 minutes, then add nut meats. Stir and serve over vanilla ice cream or pudding.

Maple Charlotte

1 tablespoon gelatine	1 cup maple syrup
¼ cup cold water	2 cups whipped cream
½ cup chopped butternuts	

Dissolve gelatine in water. Heat maple syrup and add gelatine. Chill the mixture until it thickens. Fold in whipped cream. Pour over plain cake, or serve plain in glasses. Sprinkle with nuts. Serves 6.

Maple Mousse

2 eggs, separated	1 cup maple syrup
⅛ teaspoon salt	½ pint whipped cream
1 teaspoon vanilla	

Beat egg yolks. Add salt and maple syrup. Cook in top of double boiler until mixture thickens. Cool. Fold in stiffly beaten egg whites, then cream. Add vanilla. Freeze. Serves 6.

New Englanders are continually surprised to find that the French place a high regard on the lowly mussel. We walked over uncountable acres of them in our youth, never considering them as food. They begin to appear about mid-March and are a most delicious food, properly prepared, and especially welcome during Lent. Steam them just as you would clams, and save the rapturous broth in the bottom of the kettle, thickening a bit with butter, flour, and seasoning with parsley and garlic. This delicious sauce you pour over the cooked mussels in their shells.

The mussels are scrubbed harshly before cooking, their beards removed, and rinsed with cold water.

They are also served cold on the half shell with sauce.

Sauce for Mussels

¾ cup olive oil	½ teaspoon chopped chives
¼ cup lemon juice	½ teaspoon dry mustard
½ teaspoon chopped parsley	salt and pepper

Combine the ingredients, mix well, and chill.

Mussel Omelette

3 dozen mussels	2 slices onion
4 cups water	2 tablespoons butter
1 clove garlic	1½ tablespoons chopped
pepper	parsley

4 2-egg omelettes

Scrub and debeard mussels. Cook mussels in covered pan in water seasoned with garlic and pepper for 5 minutes, or until shells open. Remove from shells. Sauté minced onion in butter in skillet. Add mussels and parsley. Toss well and fill omelettes with the mixture. Serves 4.

As if to compensate to some extent for our sacrifices, the Lenten season gives us a special treat in the form of hot cross buns. Served right from the oven, they give breakfast a holiday touch.

Hot Cross Buns

1 cup milk, scalded	3 cups flour
½ cup sugar	½ teaspoon cinnamon
3 tablespoons melted butter	½ cup currants
½ teaspoon salt	1 teaspoon grated lemon peel
1 yeast cake	1 pinch ground cloves
¼ cup warm water	1 egg, well beaten
1 egg, well beaten	confectioners' sugar and milk

Combine milk, sugar, butter, salt. When lukewarm, add yeast cake dissolved in water. Then add egg and mix well. Sift flour and cinnamon together, and stir into yeast mixture. Add currants, lemon peel, and cloves, and mix thoroughly. Cover and let rise in warm place until double in size. Shape dough into round buns and place on well-buttered baking sheet. Let rise again. Brush top of each bun with egg. Make a cross on each bun with sharp knife. Bake in hot oven (400°) for 20 minutes. Remove from oven and brush over lightly with crosses made of confectioners' sugar moistened with milk.

As the gloom of the Good Friday weekend gives way to the joy of Easter Day, we celebrate by arraying ourselves beautifully, singing enthusiastically, and dining luxuriously. For most of us, only one Easter dinner will do—the traditional Easter ham, surrounded by all the delicious trimmings.

Baked Ham

1 smoked ham	4 tablespoons ham drippings
1 cup brown sugar	cloves
1 cup bread crumbs	cherries
	pineapple slices

Place ham on rack of roasting pan and bake uncovered in a slow oven (325°), allowing 30 minutes to the pound for a whole ham. About an hour before the meat is done, remove the rind and cover the ham with a mixture of equal parts of brown sugar and bread crumbs, moistened with ham drippings. Stud the ham with cloves. Return the ham to the oven for the last hour of cooking. In the final minutes, increase the heat to 425°. Serve with cherries and pineapple slices.

Baked Ham and Fruit

2 slices baked ham	½ teaspoon cinnamon
¼ cup fruit juice or water	¼ teaspoon nutmeg
2 cups cooked peaches, pineapple, apricots, and cherries	

Sear ham in skillet. Add fruit juice or water, cover with fruit and sprinkle with spices. Cover the skillet and simmer ham for 10 minutes, basting several times. Uncover during last few minutes of cooking. Serves 4.

Sauces for Ham

RAISIN SAUCE

1 cup seedless raisins	4 tablespoons currant jelly
1 cup brown sugar	1 tablespoon lemon juice
¼ cup cider vinegar	½ teaspoon salt
4 tablespoons orange marmalade	⅛ teaspoon cloves

Cover raisins with cold water and bring to a boil. Cook until plump. Drain. Heat sugar and cider vinegar in pan. Add marmalade, jelly, lemon juice, and seasoning. Add the raisins. Heat thoroughly. Serve.

CIDER SAUCE

½ cup raisins	¾ cup orange juice
2 cups cider	½ cup brown sugar
¼ teaspoon cloves	

Plump the raisins by boiling, then drain and add to other ingredients. Simmer for 20 minutes and serve.

MUSTARD SAUCE

1 cup cream	1½ teaspoons prepared mustard
½ teaspoon salt	
⅛ teaspoon pepper	lemon juice

Mix seasonings and lemon juice, gradually stirring in the cream. Combine well. Serve.

ORANGE SAUCE

3 tablespoons butter	¼ cup vinegar
4 tablespoons flour	¼ cup brown sugar
1 cup orange juice	2 teaspoons grated orange peel
6 tablespoons sherry	2 teaspoons crystallized ginger

Melt butter. Stir in flour until browned. Add balance of ingredients and cook over low heat for 15 minutes.

Only spring could furnish us with lamb at its best, we used to think, and although "spring" lamb seems to appear the year round these days, tradition dies hard, and we still insist upon enjoying lamb more during the Easter period.

Leg of Lamb

1 5-pound leg of lamb	½ cup honey
½ cup prepared mustard	1 teaspoon salt
¼ teaspoon pepper	

Place lamb on rack in shallow roasting pan. Bake in slow oven (300°) for 2 hours. Blend mustard, honey, and seasonings, and pour over lamb. Serves 6.

Lamb Steak Casserole

2 lamb steaks, ½-inch thick	2 tomatoes, sliced
2 cloves garlic, finely chopped	1 teaspoon salt
1 cup sliced mushrooms	¼ teaspoon pepper
1 cup chopped onions	2 teaspoons paprika
1 cup chopped green pepper	½ teaspoon rosemary
¼ cup dry sherry	

Arrange lamb in shallow baking dish. Top with remaining

ingredients. Bake in slow oven (325°) for 40 minutes. Baste frequently while baking. Serves 2.

Broiled Lamb Chops

4 rib lamb chops, ¾-inch thick	2 tablespoons butter
	½ teaspoon salt
¼ cup grated Parmesan cheese	⅛ teaspoon pepper

Place the chops about 4 inches from source of heat and broil for 10-15 minutes, or until lightly browned. Turn and broil for 3 minutes. Blend cheese, butter, and seasonings. Spread on chops and broil for 2 minutes, or until cheese is slightly browned. Serves 4.

Lamb Stew

2½ pounds lamb stew meat	1 clove garlic, minced
butter	1 onion, chopped
sugar	1 stalk celery, diced
salt and pepper	2 carrots, diced
3 tablespoons flour	1 cup tomatoes
2½ cups lamb stock or water	3 cups mixed vegetables
1 bay leaf	(potatoes, peas)

Brown lamb in butter. Sprinkle with sugar. Stir in salt, pepper, and flour. Reduce heat and cook 10 minutes. Stir in stock or water and bring to boiling point. Reduce heat to simmer. Add bay leaf, garlic, onion, celery, carrots, and tomatoes. Cover tightly and simmer for 1½ hours. Sauté mixed vegetables lightly, then add to lamb. Continue cooking until lamb and vegetables are tender. Serves 6.

Cold Tomato-Lamb Cups

2 cups cooked lamb, cut in
   ½-inch cubes
3 tablespoons lemon juice
2 tablespoons olive oil
½ teaspoon paprika

½ teaspoon dry mustard
4 tomatoes
1 tablespoon mayonnaise
salt and pepper
mayonnaise

1 cucumber, thinly sliced

Combine lamb, lemon juice, olive oil, paprika, and mustard. Mix well. Chill for one hour. Remove centers from tomatoes. Chop tomato pulp and add 1 tablespoon mayonnaise, salt, and pepper. Combine with lamb mixture. Toss lightly. Fill tomato cups. Top with mayonnaise and garnish with cucumber slices. Serves 4.

Chapter 6   SPRING

April 2–May 10

THIS is the season for us. At least that is what we were telling ourselves way back there in the depth of winter when the thought of lolling under a lazy sun on a warm, sandy beach was just about all that was keeping us alive. Well, here we are. The vernal equinox has come and gone, and the first warm days of April have us gratefully complaining about spring fever.

The birds are back—bluebirds, wrens, robins galore. The pretty white shad bush is in full blossom. New shoots of green grass are forcing their way up through the old brown cover to join crocuses and daffodils. Smelt are running. It

just seems as if all of nature has become one grand stampede
to summer.

At first not too much will seem to be gained if, doggone
it, April's showers are to keep on and on. But they remind
us that the ground is giving off its cold and moisture just
now to the spring sun. There is no better way to understand
this than to seek out the hiding places of the fragrant trailing
arbutus. No, please don't pluck it—the plant is scarce enough
as is. But, brushing aside the forest floor cover, you will find
yourself asking a number of questions.

If, for example, the ground is giving off its cold to the
atmosphere—and the forest floor covering is acting as a
blanket to hold in this cold—how does this trailing arbutus
as well as other wild spring flowers bloom here earlier than
those without any such protection?

Does the ground, giving off cold, make the bed warm for
the flowers and roots of the trees? It would seem so because
all of this spring growing activity requires higher temperatures. In fact, one can almost say that where it is fifty-five
degrees, it will be spring—and there will be the spring birds,
and frogs' eggs, and skunk cabbages, and wild flowers.

The answers are not all known. The sap runs in the ever-
greens all year—no matter how cold or warm it may be. And
there are many such contradictions if you wish to take the
trouble to find them.

But to get back to this cold coming out of the ground.
You will remember how in October and November the
earth was giving out its heat, and not its cold. Just now there
is a directly opposite process. And the very same mists which

we knew last fall are now our spring mists for an exactly opposite reason. Then it was warm air coming from the ground to mix with a cold atmosphere. Now it is cold air coming up to mix with a warm day or night. In both of these processes there is the somersault—showers, or rain, or even violent storms. And, too, through this interchange come the much-feared late apple frosts when the cold north wind blasts in to join with the still cold earth, and vegetation or flowers or apple blossoms—too far advanced—are caught and destroyed.

Many early garden planters do not understand, or pay no attention to, this season when the earth is giving up its coolness. Young plants or seeds do not do well until the ground is pretty near through this discharging of the winter's cold. We have often seen peas, planted weeks later than others, come up and pass the earlier ones in the short space of three May weeks. And this spring plowing you hear so much about. There is probably as much benefit in it from the freezing of the cold soil as there is in the breaking up of clods and last year's rubble.

Doesn't it seem as if the real spring you so looked forward to last winter will never come? The last part of April and first week in May are truly exasperating that way. Really something should be done about these contrary days inside the house to make up for all the disappointments out of doors.

* * *

Persistent and dreary April's rains surely are, but they become warmer as the weeks drag by, and there is cheer in the knowledge that much of this water is needed for the vegetables and fruit of the coming season. Yes, and for the fish, too, because these rains wash bountiful nourishment for the fish into brook, river, lake, and bay.

The brook trout season begins, and the men with the feather-weight rods are off before dawn. When they return with a full creel (assuming that the fishes' appetites haven't been glutted by the floods), all should be in readiness to bring these finest of fish to the table as a memorable and savory treat.

Many people feel that the delicate flavor of trout is best preserved if you simply scale and clean the fish, and fry them in a little butter until the flesh flakes. Others, especially in the case of large trout, like to beat up an egg, dip the fish into it, and roll in salted and peppered bread crumbs before putting it into a buttered pan.

Broiled Brook Trout

4 trout
butter
salt and pepper

Wash trout (drawn) in cold water. Dry well inside and out. Brush with melted butter. Sprinkle with salt and pepper. Put fish on pre-heated broiler pan which has been greased. Broil for 5 minutes about 3 inches from heat. Broil 5 minutes on other side. Brush with melted butter several times while broiling. Serves 4.

Trout Salad

1 medium-sized lake trout	lettuce
herb vinegar	mayonnaise
4 hard-boiled eggs	

Boil trout in slightly salted water. Drain. Remove bones and skin. Break fish into flakes. Marinate in vinegar for 2 hours. Drain. Serve on lettuce leaves with mayonnaise and hard-boiled eggs. Serves 4.

Traditionally, New Englanders have taken the blooming of the shad bushes along the Connecticut River as a reliable signal that the shad were running. Invariably the blooming of the shad bushes ushered in widespread absenteeism, for baked stuffed Connecticut River shad is one of the great gourmet dishes. The shad is very bony, but, happily, for a small extra charge most fish markets will bone it for you.

Connecticut Stuffed Baked Shad

1 5-pound shad	¼ teaspoon pepper
1 cup cracker crumbs	1 small onion, minced
¼ cup melted butter	1 teaspoon sage
¼ teaspoon salt	1 cup hot water
6 strips bacon	

Clean shad and dry. Combine cracker crumbs, melted butter, salt, pepper, onion, and sage, and stuff shad. Sew edges together with needle and string. Place on a strip of clean cloth or rack in baking pan. Add water. Fasten strips of bacon on the fish with toothpicks. Bake in hot oven (400°) for 10 minutes. Then reduce heat

109

to 350° and bake for about 35 minutes, basting frequently. Serves 6.

Broiled Scrod

1 codfish	bread crumbs
salt and pepper	parsley
butter	paprika

Split a young codfish, remove bones, cut into sections for individual servings. Sprinkle with salt and pepper and dip in melted butter. Then roll in a mixture of fine bread crumbs, chopped parsley, and paprika. Place on oven-proof platter and broil until tender, about 3 inches from flame. Baste with melted butter.

Baked Mackerel

1 large mackerel	chopped chives
1 cup milk	paprika
salt and pepper	melted butter

Split and bone mackerel. Place skin down in greased pan. Pour over the mackerel, milk seasoned with salt and pepper. Bake uncovered in moderate oven (375°) for 25 minutes. Sprinkle with chopped chives and paprika. Serve with melted butter.

Baked Fillets of Haddock

4 haddock fillets	½ cup chopped onions
4 tablespoons butter	½ cup cream
	salt and pepper

Brown onions in melted butter. Add fillets and sauté. Remove fish to oven-proof dish. Add cream and seasoning to onions, and pour over the fish. Bake in moderate oven (350°) for 15 minutes. Serves 4.

Baked Haddock with Oyster Stuffing

1 4-pound haddock, dressed   1½ teaspoons salt
4 tablespoons butter, melted

Clean, wash, and dry the fish. Sprinkle with salt inside and outside. Stuff fish loosely, and sew opening with needle and string, or close with skewers. Place fish in greased baking dish. Brush with melted fat. Bake in moderate oven (350°) for 40 minutes. Remove string or skewers and serve with parsley butter. Serves 6.

OYSTER STUFFING

1 pint oysters   4 cups bread cubes, stale
½ cup celery, chopped   1 tablespoon chopped parsely
½ cup onion, chopped   1 teaspoon salt
4 tablespoons butter   ⅛ teaspoon pepper

Drain oysters, saving liquor, and chop. Cook celery and onion in butter until tender. Mix thoroughly oysters, vegetables, bread cubes, seasonings. If stuffing seems dry, moisten with oyster liquor. Sufficient for 4-pound fish.

Fillets of Sole Sautéed

4 flounder fillets   butter
½ cup milk   1 tablespoon minced
flour   summer savory
salt and pepper

Dip fillets in milk, then dust with flour, salt, and pepper. Sauté fillets in butter, turning only once. Just before serving, sprinkle lightly with savory. Serves 4.

Fresh Sardines

Cut off heads and slit. Allow to stand for an hour. Cook gently in butter, about one minute on each side.

Marinated Herring

Cover herring fillets with 2 cups sour cream, 1 cup wine vinegar. Let stand for several hours. Then chill thoroughly. Sprinkle with chives and serve on toast.

Broiled Smelts

Clean the fish. Dip in a mixture of olive oil, paprika, and bread crumbs. Broil whole. Season with salt and pepper. Serve with melted butter.

Sautéed Smelts

Clean the fish. Sprinkle with lemon juice, salt, and pepper. Cover and let stand for 15 minutes. Roll smelts in cream, dip in flour, and sauté gently in butter until done.

Baked Smelts

Clean the fish. Bake in buttered pan for 5 minutes in hot oven (450°). Serve with lemon juice, butter, and chopped chives.

Connecticut Kedgeree

2 cups cooked rice	2 tablespoons minced parsley
2 cups cooked flaked fish	½ cup top milk
4 hard-cooked eggs, chopped	salt and pepper

To hot rice add remaining ingredients and reheat in double boiler. Serve immediately. Serves 6.

Rain or shine, the days are getting warmer, and we spend more time in the open, whether fishing, bird-watching (more and more of them are checking in from the South these days), gathering herbs, or just slipping away to enjoy our spring fever unobserved.

Spring fever spent on herb gathering is far from wasted. We have learned to prize the gorgeous dandelion, the blossoms for making wine, and the leaves for boiled greens, or, raw, to give salads a little extra zip.

Dandelion Wine

4 quarts boiling water
2 quarts dandelion blossoms
3 oranges, sliced

3 lemons, sliced
1 yeast cake
4 pounds sugar

Pour boiling water over dandelion blossoms. Let it stand for three days, stirring once each day. Strain at the end of the third day. Add oranges and lemons (including peel), yeast, and sugar. Let it stand an additional three days, stirring once each day. Strain at the end of the third day. Bottle and cap. Keep for six months before using.

Dandelion Salad

dandelion greens
Boston lettuce
water cress

crisp bacon, crumbled
oil and vinegar
salt and pepper

Mix the greens, coat lightly with oil and vinegar. Add seasoning.

113

Wild Flower Combinations for Farmhouse and Village Dining Table

1. A saucer of the very first dandelions, just as a spring surprise.
2. A tall glass of purple "flags" or gentians.
3. Mayflowers or anemones, or a plate of partridge berries and their leaves.
4. A few apple blossoms from some heavily laden tree that bears poor fruit.
5. Field daisies; sometimes with grasses, sometimes with buttercups.
6. Ferns of any sort.
7. A bowl of wild roses.
8. A low glass dish filled with pond lilies.
9. A glass bowl of goldenrod with little branches of red choke berries.
10. A low bowl of scarlet bunch berries.

—from an old cookbook—

Wild Greens

Wash greens several times. Put into pan with just enough water to cover the bottom. Cook uncovered for about 5 minutes, or until tender.

Candied Sweet Flag

Clean flag root that is fully ripe. Cut into squares and boil gently in water to cover for 2½ to 3 hours. Drain. Crystallize the root sections in a boiling sugar syrup.

Sorrel Soup

1 cup sorrel leaves	2 rosemary leaves
5 tablespoons butter	salt and pepper
1 tablespoon flour	2 cups chicken stock
2 tablespoons parsley	2 egg yolks

1 cup cream

Wash sorrel; cut out center ribs; dry. Chop fine and cook in butter until of pulp consistency. Add flour, parsley, rosemary, salt, and pepper. Combine chicken stock with egg yolks and cream. Combine with sorrel mixture. Simmer for one minute. Serve with croutons. Serves 4.

Delicate and delightful native vegetables are putting in their appearance now, a new one every few weeks. Radishes add their zest to spring, eaten whole, or chopped up into salads.

Celery Stuffed with Water Cress and Roquefort

½ cup Roquefort cheese	2 tablespoons soft
¼ cup water cress, finely	butter
chopped	1 stalk celery

Blend water cress into cheese, adding butter as needed. Fill celery stalk centers and chill. Serves 4.

Scallions on Toast

12 scallions	2 pieces toast

melted butter

Cook scallions in lightly salted boiling water 20 minutes, until tender. Pour melted butter over scallions. Serve on toast. Serves 2.

115

Cucumbers are another early vegetable, refreshing and nourishing whether served with a little salt and salad dressing, boiled, baked, or pickled.

Cucumber Sauce—to serve with fish

1 cup cucumber, diced	2 teaspoons lemon juice
½ cup water	1 teaspoon grated lemon peel
2 tablespoons butter	2 teaspoons chopped dill
2 tablespoons flour	½ teaspoon salt

⅛ teaspoon pepper

Cook cucumber in water until tender. Drain, save cooking water, keep cucumber warm. Melt butter, stir in flour. Add 1 cup cooking water (adding water if necessary). Cook until thickened, stirring constantly. Stir in remaining ingredients. Add cucumber. Mix well. Yield: 2 cups.

Cucumbers with Sour Cream

2 cucumbers, peeled and sliced	2 tablespoons vinegar or
1 tablespoon salt	lemon juice
1½ cups sour cream	½ teaspoon dill

½ teaspoon pepper

Sprinkle thinly sliced cucumbers with salt and let stand for an hour. Press gently in paper to remove liquid. Mix remaining ingredients and add to cucumbers. Serves 4.

Raw Cucumber Relish

4 cucumbers, chopped fine	½ teaspoon paprika
4 tablespoons vinegar	½ teaspoon pepper
2 teaspoons salt	2 teaspoons chopped dill

Pare cucumbers, and mix with vinegar and seasonings. Yield: about 1 quart.

Bread and Butter Pickles

4 quarts cucumbers
8 small white onions, thinly
   sliced
2 green peppers, shredded
½ cup salt

5 cups sugar
1 teaspoon turmeric powder
½ teaspoon cloves
2 tablespoons mustard seed
1 teaspoon celery seed

5 cups vinegar

Wash cucumbers and slice paper-thin. Place in bowl. Add onions, peppers, and salt. Cover with a weighted lid and let stand overnight. Make a pickling syrup of the sugar and spices. Add the vinegar and pour over sliced pickles, which have been well drained and rinsed in cold water. Place over low heat and stir occasionally. Heat the mixture to scalding point but do not boil. Pour into hot sterilized jars and seal. Yield: 6 quarts.

Wonder of all the green world in spring, though, is rhubarb, and it is at its best in rhubarb pie, especially if made with the first tender stalks.

Rhubarb Pie

1 tablespoon butter
1¼ cups sugar
2 cups rhubarb, diced
2 egg yolks

1 tablespoon flour
1 8-inch pie shell
4 tablespoons sugar
2 egg whites

Melt butter, add 1 cup of the sugar and rhubarb, cook until the rhubarb is slightly softened and the sugar melted. Add egg yolks, beaten slightly. Mix the remaining ¼ cup of sugar with flour and add. Cook until rhubarb is of jelly-like consistency. Pour into baked pie shell and top with meringue made by gradually

117

beating sugar into beaten egg whites. Brown in a slow oven
(300°) about 15 minutes.

Rhubarb Tonic

2 pounds rhubarb   3 cups water

⅓ cup sugar

Wash rhubarb and cut in small pieces. Add water and cook
slowly, about 20 minutes. Strain. Add sugar, heat again to dissolve sugar. Drink when cooled.

Rhubarb Wine

4 pounds rhubarb, cut fine   4 pounds sugar
1 teaspoon almond extract   ½ yeast cake
1 gallon boiling water   ¾ tablespoon gelatine

Combine rhubarb, almond extract, and water. Let stand 3 days
and strain. Add sugar and yeast, and the gelatine dissolved in
a little water. Let stand for 2 days. Pour into jug and cork. After
three months, strain and bottle.

Rhubarb Roly Poly

2 cups flour, sifted   4 tablespoons shortening
2 teaspoons baking powder   ¾ cup milk
1 teaspoon salt   2 cups rhubarb, diced
2 tablespoons sugar   1 cup sugar

butter

Sift flour, baking powder, salt, and sugar. Cut in shortening.
Add milk. Knead on slightly floured board, and roll ⅛-inch
thick. Spread rhubarb on dough, dot generously with butter,
sprinkle with sugar, and roll like a jelly roll. Bake in moderate
(350°) oven 30 or 40 minutes. Serve with cream. Serves 6.

APRIL 2 – MAY 10

Rhubarb Bread Pudding

1 cup milk	2 cups bread crumbs
1 egg	1 tablespoon grated lemon
2 cups rhubarb, diced	rind
½ cup sugar	1 tablespoon lemon juice
	butter

Beat milk and egg well, then add rhubarb and other ingredients. Place in buttered baking dish and dot with butter. Bake in moderate oven (375°) for one hour. Serves 4.

Rhubarb and Strawberry Sauce

2 cups rhubarb, unpeeled	1 cup sugar
3 cups strawberries, hulled	

Sprinkle sugar over rhubarb, cut into small pieces. Allow to stand for several hours, then add strawberries. Cook until tender.

Rhubarb-Raspberry-Orange Conserve

4 cups rhubarb, diced	1 orange
2 cups sugar	2 cups raspberries

Sprinkle sugar over rhubarb and allow to stand overnight. Add grated rind from the orange. Then add orange slices. Mix. Add raspberries. Boil all ingredients until mixture is thick.

Chapter 7   EARLY SUMMER

May 11–June 20

THE approach of New England's so-called summer recalls the old saw, "Yes, it was a lovely summer. The day was sunny, clear, and beautiful." As with most of these old sayings, this one is not without some basis in truth. For anyone would think that by the middle of May we should be out of the winter woods, through with spring, and enjoying summer's outdoor pleasures.

Yet between May 10 and 20 we are asked to endure at least one cold spell. It is variously known as the "Dogwood Winter," or "The Time of the Three Chilly Saints," or "St. Dunston's Folly."

The dogwood, of course, is an early-flowering tree. One of

the prettiest sights in all the year is a walk down Boston's Commonwealth Avenue at this season. In practically every block, on its north side, there will be patches of lawn large enough to hold one of these dogwood trees in full bloom, and around it a display of daffodils, crocuses, and other early-flowering bulbs. The late snow or cold spell you just might catch on your trip to take in this colorful display makes a lasting memory of and belief in this "Dogwood Winter."

The Three Chilly Saints—St. Pankratus, St. Mamortus, and St. Servatius—are called "chilly" because the three days, May 11, 12, and 13, on which their martyrdom is remembered, are usually cold. The first, also known as St. Paneros, a celebrated Roman martyr, is said to have given his life for Christ at the early age of fourteen. The last made a remarkable prophecy foretelling the invasion of Huns a hundred years ahead. St. Mamortus is noted for the miracle he wrought in extinguishing the fierce fire of Vienna. None of these three saints seems to have, as does St. Swithin, for example, any direct weather connections. For once the weather is pinned onto the holy man rather than he on it.

St. Dunston, apparently a much misunderstood saint, is also connected with this cold middle-of-May spell. The legend is that he made an exchange with the devil for certain flowers. This resulted in the frost that kills the apple buds this time of year.

This little cold spell in May is known on Cape Cod as a "sheep storm." About May 15, owners of sheep take them to the shore of a pond. There they wash away the winter accumulation of filth in their wool, and shear the animals. Often a driving cold northeast storm catches the poor shorn sheep as well as their owners unaware. Such a storm might last a week or more, and if it did, it was called a sheep storm because it sickened and killed so many of the beasts. Chester Crocker, an old-timer of Marston Mills, Massachusetts, says he never heard the deacons of his church swear except during a sheep storm, and if it failed to abate after a week, this profanity would exceed the choicest of any rugged seaman.

About now, too, it is interesting to note how nature, through her climatic revolutions, is providing us with other natural foods. Although climatic change in oceans and rivers is nowhere near as severe as it is in the atmosphere, there is enough, apparently, to cause migrations among fish. These will compare in size as well as season with those of our birds. One of the most fascinating is that of the salmon. Where they go during the winter months has not been determined, but every May they are back to spawn in the upper reaches of their favorite river. Pollution, as well as factory dams, has pretty much made this return impossible in New England rivers today. But it is still to be seen in some places on the Maine and Canadian coast line.

Temperatures of land, sea, and air have so much to do with the movements and development in all kinds of wild life that we often wonder whether it is the beast or the plant that seeks out the climate, or the climate that seeks them. In studying sea bass and shad, however, it seems obvious these two fish do follow the temperature curve. The former you will find off Florida in the winter and as far north as Labrador in the summer.

And all along the beaches in between times surfcasting has, in recent years, taken a fast hold on thousands of New England fishermen. It is an engaging sport, less expensive and more romantic than that of sword or tuna fishing at sea. The beaches or rocks from which the surfcaster plies his skill are usually isolated stretches of uncommercialized scenery; off Newport, Nantucket, Provincetown, Plum Island, Old Orchard and points north, only the pounding of the breakers and the passing of small and large sea birds will interrupt the concentration of the fisherman. Out there in the currents and bottom wash beyond the breakers, who knows what he may find? Bluefish, sharks, crabs, eels, seaweed, or, perchance, a bass? The spot where he casts nevertheless will be as teeming with sea life of various kinds as are our orchards and garden plots with animal and bird life.

June in New England, although most people don't realize it, is one of the wettest months of all. This, if it is not overdone, is of course all to the good in helping the young seeds and grasses and plants in coming along. But what is more, because of all the showers and rain, it stays warm. This combination of warmth and rain is hard to beat when it comes to growing things. We envy those who have a strawberry patch at this time. Despite all the weeding and headaches of transplanting the runners, there is nothing quite equal to the year's first real dish of plump, full, ripe strawberries just off the vine served with cream.

Or fresh strawberries heaped on ice cream. The first ice-cream advertisement in the United States appeared on June

8, 1786. There probably was a good reason for a first advertisement appearing on or about that date in June. It would have to do with grasses. On an experimental farm near Williamstown, Massachusetts, the value of the early grasses—anywhere from six to twelve inches high—has long been recognized, and haying is done this time of year rather than waiting, as most farmers do, until the grass is full grown. The young grass has been found more valuable as a feed than the full-grown crop.

However, most cows out to pasture in early June get the advantage of these early grasses, and the fullness therein leads naturally to better, richer, and larger quantities of milk. Here again, as we have seen with the trailing arbutus, and the birds, and the fish of the sea, temperature is an important factor in not only sustenance and existence but a way of life as well.

"Barnaby bright, longest days and shortest nights." This is the old nursery rhyme so often quoted as the summer solstice (June 21) approaches. St. Barnabas Day used to be celebrated, before the calendar changed, on June 14—and still is. That date will do because this business of longest days and shortest nights is not a coincidence of early sunrises and late sunsets happening at the same time. Rather, as we have seen in an opposite fashion in December, at the time of the shortest days and longest nights, these June "earliest sunrises" actually are earliest (about six minutes after four) from the tenth to the twentieth, whereas the "latest sunsets" (about twenty-six minutes after seven) come on the twenty-sixth to the thirtieth.

This season from May 11 through June 20 is the perfect

occasion for the new, large, bright, and shiny picnic baskets. Toward the end of May there will be, for example, apple blossom time. We can think of at least three (and there must be many, many more) places where orchards join orchards and one can easily become lost in a wonderland of sun, blossoms, bees, and birds. The first one that comes to mind is between Littleton and Westford, Massachusetts—Route 119 is the one to take. Here is where the apple queen is chosen each June and many of the apples are stored for winter use. Another good place is between Wilton and Temple, New Hampshire, on and off Route 101. Here, in addition to the orchards, will be running brooks as well as views of the Pack Monadnock mountain range. A third place—which, from an airplane, must look at this time of year like a white blanket spread across the landscape—is between Amherst and South Hadley, Massachusetts. Here there are rolling hills, too, and the blossoming may come a little earlier than at the other two places.

But everyone knows his and her favorite apple-orchard picnic spot. There remain only the questions of the day, the blossoms, and the weather.

With the laurel, which comes along about the middle of June, one does not have to be quite so fussy about hitting the blossoms at their peak. Laurel blossoms, once out, will remain for a much longer time than those of any of the fruit trees. For your laurel-grove picnic, there are quite a few drives around New England where these groves are available and open to the public. There is a beautiful one, we are told, between Northampton and Pittsfield in the

Berkshires. One we are sure of is the state park at Townsend, Massachusetts. This is right where Route 119 joins the route which ambles between Fitchburg and Ashby. Here is a gorge with a good trout stream, many picnic tables, and a swimming pool.

Really sensitive New Englanders know the trees as their friends. Others will cut them down without so much as a wince, when a view is obstructed or a residence imperiled. But what we miss so terribly on the glaring superhighways is the kind of protective, beautiful leafy archway found over the streets of so many New England towns and cities. Groton, Massachusetts, is a good example; so is Simsbury, Connecticut. Wiscasset, Maine; Manchester, Vermont; Kingston, Rhode Island; and Hancock, New Hampshire, are other towns where stately beautiful old houses combine with the graceful trees to make unforgettable beauty.

In New England climatology the trees play an active part. Not only is their shade important, but they make admirable defenses against winds and corrosion. Ever notice how much sweeter and fresher the air is in and around forests? There is a long and complicated book in this story of New England's trees and forests with several chapters which relate to the region's climate. It should be written before all our best trees have disappeared in a cloud of sprays, hungry pulp mills, and the crookedest operators in the world—the old-time horse-trading purchaser of woodlots for their lumber.

By the end of June not only is the trees' foliage as full and fresh and green as it ever will be, but their growth is over for the year. For years one supposed that trees kept right on growing, just like everything else, all through the summer. Some years ago, however, a scientific report pointed out that June ends their growth, and personal observations since then have borne this out. How then, if tree growth ceases in June, do so many scientists find tree rings as any true measure of the weather of any given year or years? Probably the tree rings measure from about February to June, and this is all.

However, this is a time of violent thunder and lightning storms, too. So when you are out with that picnic basket, just remember that seeking out a tree for shelter could be not only dangerous but suicidal. The best place to be in such a storm is right in your car and preferably stopped where nothing can or will blow or fall upon it.

* * *

We *know* that summer is here: we feel it in the growing warmth, see it in the burgeoning trees and shrubs, and actually taste it in the many new vegetables coming from our back-yard gardens and nearby Yankee farms.

As the first asparagus spears are ready for cutting, we should give a grateful thought to Diederick Teertower, eighteenth-century Dutch consul for Massachusetts and New Hampshire, who is credited with growing the first asparagus in America, having brought over some plants from Holland and successfully raised them in West Brookfield, Massachusetts. Asparagus is one of the most versatile of vegetables, satisfying in soup, as the entree, or in the salad.

127

Fresh Boiled Asparagus

2 pounds fresh asparagus   ½ teaspoon salt
½ cup water   ⅓ cup butter
1 cup bread crumbs

Cut off or snap off the lower part of stalks, reserving these ends for the soup pot. Place stalks upright in boiling water, using lower part of double boiler. Cook asparagus covered for 15 minutes (20 minutes if you like it very tender), using top of double boiler as cover. Drain the asparagus (reserve liquor for future use). Add salt. Sauté bread crumbs in butter and pour over asparagus. Serves 4.

Creamed Asparagus

2 pounds asparagus   butter
¼ cup heavy cream   salt and pepper

Break asparagus in 1½-inch lengths, reserving tips. Place in boiling salted water. Boil for 20 minutes, adding tips the last 10 minutes of cooking. Drain, season with butter, salt, and pepper, and reheat with cream. Serves 4.

Asparagus au Gratin

2 pounds fresh asparagus   ⅓ cup butter, melted
¼ cup cheese, grated   salt and pepper

Cook asparagus for 20 minutes, drain, and place in greased oven-proof dish. Sprinkle with grated cheese. Pour melted butter over it. Season with salt and pepper. Put under broiler until cheese is browned. Serves 4.

Asparagus Amandine

2 pounds asparagus, boiled   ⅓ cup chopped almonds,
¼ cup melted butter   browned
1 tablespoon grated onion   salt and pepper

Place asparagus in shallow oven-proof dish. Mix butter and
grated onion, and pour over asparagus. Top with almonds. Put
under broiler until top browns slightly. Serves 4.

Asparagus Tips with Ham

2 pound asparagus, boiled   ¼ cup butter
4 pieces ham, thinly sliced   grated Parmesan cheese
              ¼ cup melted butter

Wrap each piece of ham around three stalks of cooked asparagus.
Place in buttered baking dish, dot with ¼ cup butter. Sprinkle
generously with cheese. Place dish in hot oven (400°) for 5
minutes. Sprinkle with melted butter and serve. Serves 4.

Aside from that brief cold spell in the middle of May,
we are now coming into perfect picnic weather. A warm sun
has sponged up the mud puddles and caused flowers to pop
out of the ground. The days grow longer and more beautiful.

One dish can ensure the culinary success of all the week-
ends, the parties, and picnics of the entire summer: ice
cream. Just make a weekend habit of whipping up a freezer-
ful (the good old-fashioned way) of ice cream, and you'll
find family and friends delighted to extemporize with chocolate, honey, maple syrup, chopped nuts, preserved fruits,

129

and all manner of delicious and decorative ingredients. If other parts of the meal have failed to reach an orbit, all its shortcomings will be forgotten during the ice-cream jamboree.

Vanilla Ice Cream

1 cup cream	⅛ teaspoon salt
1 cup sugar	3 cups cream
1½ teaspoons vanilla	

Heat 1 cup cream very slowly (do not boil). Then stir in sugar and salt until dissolved. Chill. Add 3 cups cream and vanilla, and freeze. Makes 1½ quarts.

Peach Ice Cream

4 pounds ripe peaches, pared and sliced	⅛ teaspoon salt
	1 teaspoon vanilla
1 cup sugar	4 cups cream

Mash peaches and stir in half the sugar. Add salt. Let stand until sugar dissolves. Then add balance of sugar, vanilla, and cream. Freeze. Makes 1½ quarts.

Rhubarb Ice Cream

2½ pounds rhubarb, cut up	2½ cups sugar
2 cups water	⅛ teaspoon salt
4 cups heavy cream, whipped	

Boil rhubarb in water for 10 minutes. Add sugar, salt. Cool, then add cream. (For creamy texture, let stand overnight.) Pack in ice-cream freezer in finely chopped ice and rock salt. Freeze. Yield: about 2 quarts.

Ice Cream

AND

. . . cantaloupe

. . . stewed hot apricots or prunes

. . . strawberries, raspberries, blueberries, peaches—your favorite fruit

. . . sour cream mixed with cinnamon, nutmeg, and sugar

. . . hot maple syrup
(boil syrup for 5 minutes and add toasted almonds)

. . . fruit and rum sauce
(combine equal parts of puréed fruit and orange juice; flavor with rum)

. . . orange marmalade sauce
(combine ¾ cup orange marmalade with ½ cream)

. . . crème de menthe

. . . marshmallow sauce
(boil ¾ cup sugar and ¼ cup milk until thread forms. Melt ½ pound marshmallows in 2 tablespoons water in double boiler. Combine. Beat until smooth)

Coconut Ice Cream

2 cups shredded coconut	⅓ cup sugar
1½ cups milk	1 cup whipping cream
1 tablespoon gelatine	1 cup light cream
2 tablespoons water	1 teaspoon vanilla

Combine 1⅓ cups coconut with milk. Allow to stand for 30 minutes, then simmer for 10 minutes. Cool and strain the mixture through several thicknesses of cheesecloth, squeezing out as much liquid as possible. Discard the remainder. Soak gelatine in water for 10 minutes. Reheat coconut liquid, and dissolve gelatine in it. Chill and whip cream, add light cream, vanilla, gelatine, strained coconut milk. Stir in remaining ⅔ cup shredded coconut and freeze. Yield: 1 quart.

Coconut Cake

SPONGE CAKE

2 cups sugar
8 eggs

2 cups flour, sifted
grated rind—1 lemon
1 cup melted butter

Beat sugar, eggs, and lemon peel in top of double boiler until lukewarm. Remove from heat and beat until cold. Gently add flour and melted butter. Place in buttered and flour-dusted pan and bake in moderate oven (350°) for 40-45 minutes.

CREAM FILLING

8 eggs yolks, beaten
1¼ cups sugar
¾ cup flour

1 teaspoon cornstarch
1 vanilla bean (or ½
teaspoon vanilla extract)
4 cups milk, scalded

Beat egg yolks. Mix with sugar. Then add flour and cornstarch. Gradually add milk, flavored with vanilla. Cook all together for a minute, stirring constantly.

MARSHMALLOW FROSTING

¼ pound marshmallows
2 tablespoons hot water

1 cup sugar
½ cup coconut milk
1 teaspoon vanilla

Cut marshmallows into small pieces and melt in double boiler. Add water and cook until smooth. Heat sugar and coconut milk slowly, bring to boiling point without stirring. Allow to boil for 6 minutes. Add slowly to marshmallow mixture, stirring

constantly until well mixed and smooth. Beat until cool enough
to spread. Then add vanilla.

NOTE: Coconut milk is made by putting grated coconut into
milk and boiling for a few minutes. Strain and discard
coconut.

When sponge cake is cool, split into halves and fill with cream
filling. Sprinkle with grated coconut. Put other half on top and
press slightly. Spread marshmallow frosting very thickly over
entire cake, then press grated coconut into it. Place in refrigerator
for an hour before slicing it.

And there's the wonderful summertime world of strawberries:

Strawberries in a Barrel

Who can help being thrilled by the idea of a barrel that
spurts out luscious red strawberries at every angle of the
compass? Just picture a barrel practically clothed in strawberries!

Here's how to have one of your own. Just get hold of a
good-sized barrel and paint the entire outside with a reliable wood preservative. Then drill holes, an inch or two in
diameter, in the barrel, leaving twelve or fourteen inches
from one to another.

Irrigation of the barrel is provided by centering in it a
length of stovepipe four to six inches in diameter, fixed
vertically—and filled with gravel, crushed stone, or cinders.
Then fill in all around the stovepipe with earth; a sandy
loam is best. Now ease out the stovepipe, leaving the porous

material as a means of feeding water to the surrounding area.

Then put your strawberry plants into the drilled holes in the barrel, giving them a tender tucking in, and cheering the proceedings by the addition of liquid plant food.

Your barrel should be established where it will benefit daily from a full charge of sunlight, and you must, of course, do your part by frequent watering of the central column of porous material. Planting should be done before the end of June.

Strawberry Ice Cream

4 cups strawberries   1 cup sugar
                    4 cups cream

Crush strawberries and stir in sugar. Chill. Add cream. Freeze. Yield: about 2 quarts.

Strawberries and Rhubarb

4 cups rhubarb   8 cups sugar
                    8 cups strawberries

Cut rhubarb in small pieces and sprinkle sugar over it. Allow to stand overnight. In the morning, bring quickly to a boil and add strawberries. Boil until thick, 15 or 20 minutes. Serves 8.

Strawberry Sandwich

3 eggs, separated	¼ teaspoon salt
8 tablespoons sugar	1 cup strawberries
1 tablespoon hot water	½ cup heavy cream, whipped
6 tablespoons flour	3 tablespoons sugar
1 teaspoon baking powder	½ teaspoon vanilla

Beat egg whites stiffly, reserving one egg white. Add one yolk. Beat mixture for 3 minutes. Follow the same procedure as other two yolks are added. Then add sugar and hot water, and beat 5 minutes. Sift flour, baking powder, and salt. Stir lightly. Pour mixture into two small cake tins and bake for 15 minutes in hot oven (375°). Cool.

Mash the strawberries with a fork. Beat one egg white until stiff, and fold into the whipped cream. Add sugar and strawberries gradually. Add vanilla. Spread one cake with strawberry filling and place the other cake on top. Serves 2.

Strawberry Shortcake

2 cups flour	½ cup butter
3 teaspoons baking powder	¾ cup milk
1 teaspoon salt	2 quarts strawberries, sliced
3 teaspoons sugar	1½ cups sugar
whipped cream	

Mix and sift dry ingredients. Cut in butter. Add milk to form a soft dough. Pat lightly on floured board to form two cakes ½-inch thick. Bake in a hot oven (450°) for 15 minutes. Add sugar to sliced strawberries. Butter the cakes, spreading berries on each layer, and topping the dish with whipped cream. Serves 6.

Dipped Strawberries

3 cups sugar	1 cup cold water
strawberries	

Prepare fondant by stirring sugar and water over low heat until sugar is dissolved. Cook quickly, without stirring, to the soft ball stage. Pour the syrup onto a buttered platter, and when cool, stir it with a fork, clockwise, and working from the outside toward the center. When the syrup creams, knead it with the hands, then cover with a damp cloth and let stand for 15 minutes.

When ready to dip strawberries, reheat 4 tablespoons of fondant in double boiler and add a drop of vanilla. Hold berries by their stems and dip individually into fondant, then turn up so that the fondant will run down to the stem. Place on cold cookie pan covered with wax paper.

The unused fondant may be put in airtight container and stored in refrigerator for future use.

Strawberry Custard

4 eggs	1 cup scalded milk
¼ cup sugar	1 teaspoon brandy or vanilla
⅛ teaspoon salt	2 cups heavy cream

2 cups strawberries, washed and chilled

Beat egg yolks slightly, then add sugar and salt. Stir in the scalded milk slowly, and place over very low heat until custard begins to thicken. Stir in brandy and let cool. When ready to serve, whip cream and fold in beaten egg whites. Fold in the custard and strawberries. Serves 4.

Strawberry Preserves

8 cups strawberries	1 teaspoon lemon juice
4 cups sugar	4 cups sugar

Wash strawberries and cover with boiling water for about 3 minutes. Drain and add 4 cups sugar and 1 teaspoon lemon juice. Boil for 15 minutes. Add 4 cups sugar. Boil for additional 5 minutes. Let berries stand overnight. Pour into sterilized glasses and seal.

Summer keeps a-cumin' in with new and delicious vegetables.

Boiled Carrots

Wash 8 carrots and boil in small quantity of boiling water, cooking for 20 minutes, or until done. Skin. Add seasoning. Cover with melted butter and sprinkle with chopped parsley. Serves 4.

Honey Glazed Carrots

Wash and scrape 8 carrots. Boil in small quantity of boiling water for about 20 minutes, or until done. Drain. Add 4 tablespoons butter and ¼ cup honey to pan. Simmer until carrots are glazed. Serves 4.

Carrots and Green Peas

Boil carrots as indicated above. Combine with boiled green peas. Drain. Season with salt and pepper. Cover with melted butter and serve with chopped parsley.

Green Peas with Mint

Wash and hull 2 cups of peas. Boil until tender. Serve with 4 tablespoons melted butter to which 2 tablespoons of chopped mint leaves have been added.

Green Peas and Lettuce

Wash and hull 2 cups of peas. Place in top of double boiler. Cover with lettuce leaves and cook covered until tender. Remove the lettuce leaves. Add butter, salt, and pepper to the peas. Serve peas with chopped parsley.

137

Harvard Beets

1 tablespoon cornstarch	¼ cup vinegar
4 tablespoons sugar	¼ cup water
½ teaspoon salt	2 tablespoons butter
2 cups cooked beets, sliced	

Mix cornstarch, sugar, and salt. Add vinegar and water. Boil gently until thick, stirring constantly. Add butter and beets. Reheat and serve. Serves 4.

Beets in Cranberry Sauce

2 cups cranberries	4 tablespoons honey
1 cup orange juice	2 bunches beets, boiled

Boil cranberries in orange juice until soft, then mash through sieve. Add honey and heat cooked, skinned beets in sauce. Serves 4.

Baked Beets

12 medium-sized beets	melted butter
1 cup green onions	salt and pepper

Wash beets and bake in moderate (350°) oven for 30 minutes. Turn down heat to 325° and bake another 25 minutes. When tender, peel and put in saucepan with melted butter, salt and pepper, and minced green onion. Serves 4.

Beets Baked in Honey

8 beets, cooked	1 teaspoon grated orange peel
2 tablespoons butter	½ cup honey
¼ cup orange juice	salt and pepper

Dice beets and place in pan. Add other ingredients. Cook over moderate heat until glaze forms on beets. Serves 4.

Fruit and Vegetable Salad

1 cup apples, sliced	1 cup carrots, diced
1 cup peaches, sliced	½ cup raisins
1 cup pears, sliced	½ cup cabbage, chopped
1 cup celery, diced	¼ cup onion, finely minced

½ cup walnuts

Combine these ingredients. Delicious with either French dressing or mayonnaise. Serves 6.

Chapter 8 SUMMER

June 21–August 1

PERHAPS the reason New England trees have stopped growing at just the time when many summer crops are beginning has something to do with trees—at least their crowns—being higher off the ground. Thus far we have concerned ourselves much more with ground temperatures and that of lakes, oceans, and mists than we have with the masses of air above these. It is the ten-thousand-foot level, meteorologists say, that really makes New England weather.

We know, for example, that the higher up one goes, the colder the weather becomes. We know also that up there the winds blow with considerably more force than they do at surface levels. It is something like one degree lower temperature for every five hundred feet of elevation, and the wind has been measured from the top of Mount Washington in New Hampshire at two hundred and thirty-five miles per hour. Other conditions being normal, then, New England is capped with a cold ceiling all year. Most of it moves from southwest to northeast, in keeping with the earth's rotation, at a very high speed.

July is a good time for observing in the formation, approach, and dissolution of the thunderheads at least a part of this upper-versus-lower air chemistry. Tons of cool moisture are carried in the billowing white clouds, soon to be freed by the rising hot air mass in which we are living, and dumped upon us. Just so come the changes in New England fall and winter temperatures from similar meetings between Arctic cold air masses and those rising toward it from the tropical states.

It is a mixed-up mess and not understood completely by any man or woman, alive or dead—at least to the point of usefulness in forecasting the weather. Anyhow, whatever combination of forces keeps this ceiling of cold from descending upon us works just fine at this particular season. From the summer solstice of June 21 through the first of August, we can be reasonably certain that, barring occasional showers or rain, it will be warm, and most likely hot.

For those who find their fun mostly on shore during these hot July weeks, perhaps the real highlight of the summer will turn out to be a well-done beach party or clambake. A lot of the paraphernalia for either one can be lugged along from home, and often is. Yet half the fun of these for us has been the finding of a good isolated location and arriving early enough on the scene to begin right at the beginning with the very first chore—that of collecting firewood for the fire.

There are quite a few places along the New England coast where such isolation is accessible. One that comes to mind is the beach off Orleans, Cape Cod, where Henry Beston wrote his American classic, "The Outermost House." You can drive, especially in a jeep or with balloon tires, almost to the end of it. And there one finds not only an outer beach with tremendous waves crashing ashore day and night, but also an inner beach, relatively calm, and safe enough for even small children. In between the two beaches are high and low dunes. Passes here and there connect the beaches. So, no matter which way the wind blows, your beach party will find a quiet spot for the fire, all the fancy food and fixin's.

For less adventurous souls or those who don't have time to get to a place for a real "bake," almost any public beach will provide a nook behind a breakwater. On a calm night the open beach itself is good. At the full moon this sort of mild eating out can be pretty and romantic, too. Have you ever seen the millions of little hands that seem to reach up out of the sea as the moon slowly rises over it? Or followed the course of lighted steamers toward the moon's beam path? Or watched Minot's Light, off Cohasset and Scituate, Massachusetts, flash its famous "I Love You" signal—1, 4, then 3?

We cannot leave the sea, of course, until we have had our fill, too, of the fresh sea foods there. There will be lobsters, and lobsters done in many different ways. Our favorite place

142

for these happens to be at Pemaquid Point in Maine. There near the old fort is a T-shaped restaurant—the long end of the T being a walkway to the end of the dock. Here one orders clams and lobsters and, while they are being boiled in fresh sea water, one returns to the short part of the T for melted butter, napkins, potato chips, coffee, and whatever else may be chosen for the meal. By that time, the clams are ready and you find a long table on the dock over the water—all your own—and the feast is on. Then your lobsters are announced and you carry these to your table, too. At no other place have we known clams and lobsters to melt in our mouths the way these do here—nor to be as reasonable— or served in a more delightful and beautiful New England setting.

There is something about Maine weather this time of year, too, that gives an added zing to the appetite. Some say this arises from the combination of fir trees and the sea—these two combining to make a particularly healthful ozone mixture. Others think it is found in Maine's cold ocean water— making for warm days and always cool evenings.

But one doesn't have to drive all the way to Maine to find good lobster eating places. The whole New England coast line is dotted with them in the summer from Maine to Connecticut.

Thousands upon thousands of New Englanders are taking advantage of the river-and-lake small-boat craze. The disease begins in one of two ways: the innocent victim inherits or buys a camp on a lake, or he purchases a boat and outboard motor. The latter is usually the villain in the piece. Some say it bears a psychological relationship to man in the same way an automobile does—the faster and bigger it is, the more the man driving it feels himself a potent, magnificent force. How many will tell you, frankly, they don't know why it is but when they had three-horsepower motors, they changed them for five-horsepower, and so on up until they were in the forty-, fifty- and even 60-horsepower class.

For those who wish to do their camping at home—either in the mountains or at the seashore—the outdoor fireplace has taken on in a truly big way. It will be seen in various guises—all the way from a steel wheelbarrow in which logs have somehow been induced to burn, to truly magnificent electrical pushcarts set to burn charcoal fires and, if you wish, an oven for baking, too. "You pays your money and you takes your choice."

* * *

It may be a certain temperature, a kind of dryness in the air, or, more likely, a combination of such tangibles with atavistic mysteries, that leads one to return to nature: one suddenly has an irresistible urge to cook as one's ancestors did twenty thousand years ago, out-of-doors. This is the season for it.

A grill on bricks in the back yard, a mason-built fireplace on a terrace, a clambake, a barbecue, or a beach party, all have the same general principles, and the general satisfaction is as certain.

Family excitement builds up to a real pitch with the planning of a barbecue—in the back yard or elsewhere—and New Englanders are rather partial to chicken as well as the usual frankfurters and steak. Aside from any tenuous remnants of sentiment because our earliest forebears of the Massachusetts Bay Colony survived through their first bitter winters on the birds of the forest, barbecued chicken is just—well—delicious.

Barbecued Chicken

Split chickens down the back (allowing half a chicken for each person). Brush with melted butter and place on broiling rack with the skin side down, about 5 inches from the heat. Broil for 15 minutes, brush with butter, then turn and broil the other side. Repeat the process, so that the chickens broil about an hour altogether. Baste from time to time with barbecue sauce during the last 30 minutes.

Grilled Fruits for the Barbecue

BANANAS

Place bananas, unpeeled, on grill over hot coals. Cook for 7 or 8 minutes on each side. Serve in skin.

PEARS

Dip pears in honey. Cook on grill over hot coals until thoroughly heated. Serve with honey.

ORANGES

Dip orange slices in butter. Place over hot coals and brown quickly on each side.

PINEAPPLE

Sprinkle pineapple slices with a little rum. Place over hot coals and heat thoroughly.

145

PEACHES

Dip peach halves in melted butter. Roll in brown sugar, to which ginger or other spices have been added. Broil over hot coals for 10 minutes.

MIXED FRUIT

Cut fresh fruit in chunks or slices and marinate for 2 hours in a mixture of kirsch and honey. Arrange fruit on skewers and broil over hot coals for 10 minutes. When done, sprinkle with lemon juice.

Grilled Vegetables for the Barbecue

TOMATOES

Brush tomato halves with butter, sprinkle with chopped basil or dill, and bread crumbs. Broil over coals until tomatoes are lightly browned.

POTATOES

Roast potatoes in aluminum foil. When done, break open and serve with sour cream and a sprinkling of dill.

CORN

Pull back corn husks so that silk can be removed, dip ears in cold water, and push back the husks. Roast on grill for about 20 minutes, turning often.

SWEET POTATOES

Parboil potatoes in their jackets. Peel and cut into thick slices. Cook over hot coals, turning frequently, until golden brown.

ONIONS

Cut large onions in 1-inch-thick slices. Dip in melted butter. Cook over hot coals until golden brown on both sides. Sprinkle with salt and pepper.

Outdoor cookery reaches its greatest glory, of course, in the classic clambake, whose formula differs only slightly from one community to another—and has changed little since the Indians were masters of the North American continent and gorged themselves in seaside celebrations.

A well-regulated clambake starts off properly with clam chowder. Here again recipes differ only slightly except for an outlaw version that contaminates the chowder by mixing in tomatoes.

Clam Chowder

1 quart shucked clams	½ teaspoon salt
¼ pound salt pork, diced	⅛ teaspoon pepper
2 onions, finely sliced	4 cups milk
6 medium-sized potatoes, sliced thin	2 tablespoons butter

Rinse clams in clam liquor. Remove black caps. Strain and reserve ½ cup clam liquor. Chop clams and set aside. Fry salt pork until brown and crisp. Drain on paper. Sauté onion slices, then add potatoes. Sprinkle with salt and pepper. Sauté for 10 minutes. Add chopped clams and ½ cup clam liquor. Cover with water and cook for 20 minutes. Add fried pork and fat to clams and vegetables. Then heat milk and add to the chowder. Add butter, season to taste, and serve. Serves 8.

While the clam chowder is a separate course, clam broth is served as an accompaniment to the rest of the "bake."

Clam Broth

1 quart clams	2 cups cold water

Scrub clams and rinse several times until free from sand. Place clams in large kettle, add water, and cover. Cook over low heat for 20 minutes. Remove clams from broth. Let stand so that liquor can settle. Strain. Serve hot or cold. Serves 6.

Classic Clambake

The clambake itself can be really thrilling. A level spot should be found above the high-tide level. Roundish stones about a foot in diameter are collected and spread out so they cover a circular area about a yard in diameter. Have this base a little higher in the center.

Now build a good hot fire on top of the stones and keep it roaring for about two hours when the stones should be white hot. Rake away all the coals and ashes, and cover the stones with about a six-inch layer of rockweed—the kind of seaweed that has little air bubbles in it.

You have ready at hand little (quart-size) bags made of cheesecloth. Some are filled with clams, some with potatoes, some fish, some new sweet corn (outside husk should be removed). Tie the bags low enough so you will have a good handle when the time comes to get them out of the scalding seaweed. Bags large enough to hold several pound or pound-and-a-quarter lobsters will make their handling simpler.

On the first layer of rockweed distribute your bags of corn and lobster, alternating and placing in neat circles for appearance's sake. Different colored cheesecloth can add to this effect.

Cover this layer with rockweed, and lay on the bags of fish, shellfish, and potatoes. Basically, this is just a way of steaming food, but it is a wonderful way because of the salt and herby steam that comes from the rockweed, and even more because of the communion of sea-food odors and flavors.

Over all you lay a sheet of wet canvas which you keep wet during the next forty-five minutes of baking.

There you have the classic pattern, and as in all other recipes, you should follow it a time or two, and then go off on your own, deviating, adding, subtracting, and perhaps discovering! Chicken split in half, oysters, mussels, whatever you think would steam well—try them at your clambake.

Thrilling? Directions seldom are, but one assumes that this is all happening on a wide expanse of golden sand, combed at the edges by the foam of a blue sea—and all under the deep blue canopy of a sky serene save for the curvettings of a few hungry gulls. With the canvas in place, the bake assumes the aspect of a prehistoric pyre, and the beach takes on a timelessness deliciously spiced by escaping steam. That's a Yankee clambake!

Rhode Island Quahog Chowder

⅛ pound salt pork, diced
2 onions, sliced
5 potatoes, diced

1 quart boiling water
½ pint quahogs, drained
liquor from quahogs

salt and pepper

Fry salt pork until brown and crisp. Add onions and potatoes. Sauté for about 5 minutes. Add this mixture to kettle of boiling water. Cook about 20 minutes, or until potatoes are done. Add finely cut quahogs. Add some of the liquor from quahogs for added flavoring. Season and simmer for 5 minutes, or until quahogs are cooked. Serves 6.

Yankee Clam Chowder

¼ pound salt pork, diced	2 cups boiling water
2 medium-sized onions, diced	1 quart clams, chopped, and
3 cups potatoes, diced	juice
½ teaspoon salt	1 quart milk
¼ teaspoon pepper	2 tablespoons butter
1 pint light cream	

Cook pork until crisp, add onions, and cook 5 minutes. Mix in potatoes, seasonings, and water. Cover and simmer for 15 minutes. Add clams and their liquor; then milk, butter, and cream. Heat and serve. Serves 8.

Boiled Lobster

Put live lobster, head first, into boiling sea water or salted water. Allow enough water to cover lobster completely. Bring water to a boil again and cook lobster 20 to 25 minutes, depending upon size. Split lengthwise, remove inedible portions, and serve with melted butter.

Broiled Lobster

Split lobster from tail to head, then flatten, shell side down, crack large claws, brush with melted butter, season with salt and pepper. Broil small lobsters 6 minutes under hot flame, larger lobsters 15 or 20 minutes. Serve with melted butter.

Baked Lobster

Split lobsters and prepare as for broiling (above). Place in shallow pan in hot oven (450°) and bake for 20 minutes. Baste frequently with melted butter. Season with salt and pepper. Serve with melted butter.

Fried Lobster

Dip pieces of boiled lobster meat into beaten egg and 'roll in corn meal. Fry in deep vegetable fat until brown. Serve with tartar sauce.

Lobster Newburg

2 cups boiled lobster meat	2 egg yolks
2 tablespoons butter	1 cup cream
½ teaspoon paprika	¼ cup sherry
salt and pepper	toast

Dice lobster and heat with butter in double boiler or chafing dish. Cook 3 or 4 minutes, then add seasonings. Beat egg yolks with cream, pour over lobster, and cook until the mixture thickens. Stir, do not permit to boil. Remove from fire. Add sherry, serve on hot buttered toast or crackers.

Our Pilgrims got through more than one chill and desolate winter because they were settled on the rim of an ocean full of fish and largely surrounded by shellfish. Among these latter, crabs were fairly easy to capture, were very nourishing, and could be delicious in many ways.

Deviled Crabs

3 tablespoons butter	3 cups crab meat, freshly cooked
4 tablespoons flour	4 yolks of hard-cooked eggs
½ teaspoon salt	2 tablespoons chopped parsley
⅛ teaspoon pepper	½ teaspoon nutmeg
1½ cups milk	

1 cup buttered bread crumbs

Melt butter over low heat. Add flour, salt, and pepper. Stir until well blended, then remove from heat. Gradually stir in milk and return to fire. Cook, stirring constantly, until thick and smooth, about 2 minutes. Take from fire and add crab meat, broken into small pieces, mashed egg yolk, parsley, and nutmeg. Put mixture in buttered shallow baking dish. Cover with bread crumbs. Bake in moderate oven (375°) 20 or 30 minutes. Serves 8.

Sautéed Soft-Shell Crabs

Wash and clean crabs. Dredge with flour and salt. Sauté in butter, about 2 minutes on each side. Serve with lemon juice and butter from the pan.

Crab Meat Mousse

2 cups cooked crab meat
¾ cup cracker crumbs
4 eggs
1 cup milk
¼ cup butter
¼ teaspoon finely chopped
    garlic
1 teaspoon Worcestershire
    sauce

1 tablespoon finely chopped
    onion
1 tablespoon finely chopped
    chives
2 teaspoons baking powder
salt and pepper
2 cups cream sauce
curry powder

Mix ingredients in the order given. Stir well. Grease a ring mold with butter, and pour in crab mixture. Place mold in pan of boiling water. Place in slow oven (325°) and bake for 45 minutes. Serve with cream sauce to which has been added a sprinkling of curry powder.

Toward the end of June a miraculous thing comes to pass: a delightful kind of birth, the arrival of the first young peas, and this ushers in a famous New England dish.

One of the greatest misdirections in the entire lexicon of cooking is the reference everywhere to "boiled salmon and peas" as the traditional and required dish for the Fourth of July in New England. So far as I know, this dish has never been served in New England on the Fourth of July. New Englanders do speak of "boiled salmon." What they serve, of course, is poached salmon. Actually the fish is simmered, and it is very important not to boil it.

"Boiled" Salmon

1 3-pound salmon	2 quarts court bouillon
	2 cups egg sauce

Wrap salmon in cheesecloth. Place in kettle and cover with sufficient court bouillon to cover fish. Bouillon should be boiling when salmon is immersed, then reduce heat immediately and simmer fish about 8 minutes to each pound. Do not permit bouillon to boil. Drain salmon and serve with egg sauce. Serves 6.

COURT BOUILLON

⅓ cup chopped carrots	2 bay leaves
⅓ cup chopped celery	6 cloves
⅓ cup chopped onions	6 peppercorns
3 tablespoons butter	½ cup red wine vinegar
1 tablespoon minced parsley	2 quarts boiling water

Sauté vegetables in butter for 5 minutes. Add remaining ingredients and simmer 5 minutes. Bring to boil. (Put unused bouillon in sealed jar in a cool place for future use.)

EGG SAUCE

4 tablespoons butter   2 cups milk
4 tablespoons flour   salt and pepper
2 hard-cooked eggs

Melt butter. Blend in flour very slowly. Add milk gradually. Season with salt and pepper. Add finely cut eggs. Yield: 2 cups.

Along with this will be served

New Potatoes in Cream

6 small new potatoes   ½ cup minced shallots
1 cup cream   ¼ cup chopped parsley
salt and pepper

Scrub potatoes. Boil 5 minutes. Drain. Bake in moderate (350°) oven until done. Heat cream and stir in shallots, parsley, seasoning. Pour over potatoes (unpeeled), cut in quarters. Serves 2.

Berries with all their color and flavor are part of the glory of this season. Blueberries are especially delicious, and never more so than in a pudding that Cape Codders call "Blueberry Grunt" and Mainlanders call:

Blueberry Slump

2 cups blueberries   1 cup flour, sifted
½ cup sugar   2 teaspoons baking powder
1 cup water   ¼ teaspoon salt
½ cup milk

Stew blueberries, sugar, and water for 10 minutes. Mix and sift flour, baking powder, and salt. Add milk, stirring quickly to

154

form a dough to drop from end of spoon. Drop into the boiling sauce and cook 10 minutes with cover off, 10 minutes with cover on. Serve with cream. Serves 4.

Maine Blueberry Muffins

2 cups flour	1 egg, well beaten
2½ teaspoons baking powder	¾ cup milk
¾ cup sugar	¼ cup melted fat
½ teaspoon salt	1 cup blueberries

Sift flour, then measure. Add baking powder, sugar, and salt, and sift again. Add egg and milk to flour mixture and stir. Add shortening. Fold in blueberries. Bake in greased muffin tins in a hot oven (400°) for 25 to 30 minutes. Yield: 1 dozen.

Blueberry Upside-Down Cake

2 tablespoons butter	6 tablespoons blueberry syrup
1 cup brown sugar	1 cup flour, sifted
½ cup blueberry syrup	1 teaspoon baking powder
1 cup cooked blueberries	1 teaspoon salt
3 egg yolks	3 egg whites
1 cup sugar	whipped cream

Heat butter, sugar, and blueberry syrup for 5 minutes. Place berries in bottom of 10-inch baking dish and cover with syrup. In a separate bowl, beat together egg yolks, sugar, and 6 tablespoons blueberry syrup. Add sifted flour, baking powder, and salt. Fold in beaten egg whites. Pour the batter over the blueberries and bake in moderate oven (350°) for 40 minutes. Serve upside down. Top with whipped cream. Serves 6.

Blueberry Crisp

4 cups blueberries	1 tablespoon lemon juice
¾ cup sugar	2 cups bread crumbs
½ teaspoon cinnamon	2 tablespoons Bleu cheese,
¼ teaspoon salt	crumbled

2 tablespoons melted butter

Combine berries, sugar, seasonings, and lemon juice. Combine bread crumbs, butter, and cheese. In a greased 1-quart casserole, alternate layers of berry mixture and bread-crumb mixture, ending with the latter. Cover and bake in hot oven (400°) for 15 minutes. Uncover and bake a few minutes longer, until crumbs are brown. Serve warm. Serves 6.

Blueberry Bread-and-Butter Pudding

8 thin slices white bread	1 cup sugar
¼ cup butter	pinch of salt
4 cups blueberries	1 cup whipped cream

Remove crusts from bread and butter each slice, using all the butter. Stew berries, sugar, and salt for 15 minutes. Arrange alternate slices of bread and stewed berries in buttered baking dish. Bake in moderate oven (350°) for 20 minutes. Serve cold with whipped cream. Serves 6.

A flavor that is entirely individual, and bears no relationship to any other, is that of the raspberry, a relaxed red with a relaxed flavor.

Raspberry Cream

4 cups raspberries	3 cups boiling water
1 cup sugar	2 tablespoons cornstarch

Put raspberries and sugar into boiling water. Boil for 3 minutes. Mix cornstarch with small amount of cold water. Stir into the mixture and bring again to boiling point. Serve cold with cream. Serves 4.

With the blazing up of the summer sun, refreshing drinks are much in demand. No summer drink could be more delicious and thirst-quenching than lemonade, but there are other good drinks for a change.

Raspberry Cooler

2 cups water   2 cups raspberry juice
½ cup powdered sugar   ½ cup lemon

Combine sugar and water. Add raspberry juice and lemon juice. Mix. Serve over cracked ice.

Raspberry Float

1 quart milk, chilled   2 cups crushed raspberries
6 tablespoons honey   ½ teaspoon almond extract
1 quart vanilla ice cream

Combine all ingredients. Beat until blended. Pour into chilled glasses. Serves 6.

Raspberry Royal

3 quarts ripe raspberries   white sugar
1 quart cider vinegar   brandy

Combine fruit and vinegar, and let stand for 24 hours. Then put into flannel or muslin bag, squeeze and strain. For each pint of

157

liquid allow 1 pound of sugar. Boil half an hour in large kettle, skimming constantly until clear. When cool, add ½ cup brandy to each quart of shrub. Bottle and seal.

Sherry Cobbler

Half fill a tall glass with crushed ice. Add a tablespoon of powdered sugar and a sherry glass of sherry for each serving. Stir until glass is frosted. Garnish with cherry.

Never in New England was there a haying without quantities of cold switchel at hand. Men working in the fields could drink any amount of it without cloying the taste or destroying the appetite. Even if it became tepid, it was still refreshing.

Haymakers' Switchel

2 quarts water	½ cup molasses
1 cup sugar	½ cup vinegar
	½ teaspoon ginger

Just stir up the ingredients and cool. Old-time custom was to pour it into a stone jug and lower the jug into the well.

Spiced Milk

2 quarts milk, scalded	½ teaspoon nutmeg
1½ teaspoons cinnamon	3 tablespoons sugar

Mix spices and sugar with small quantity of milk. Gradually add balance of milk. Serve hot or cold. Serves 8.

Coffee Frosted

2 cups cold coffee   1 cup pineapple juice
1 pint coffee ice cream

Combine coffee and pineapple juice. Add ice cream and beat well. Serve with whipped cream. Serves 4.

Iced Tea and Rum

Combine strong tea with rum, add sugar to taste. Garnish with a sprig of mint.

Pimm's Cup

Fill pewter mug with 2 jiggers of Pimm's #1 Cup. Add ice and strip of cucumber. Fill mug with ginger ale.

Mocha Punch

4 cups cold coffee	⅛ teaspoon salt
1 quart chocolate ice cream	2 cups whipped cream
½ teaspoon almond extract	nutmeg

Pour coffee into large punch bowl. Add half of the ice cream and beat until the ice cream melts slightly. Add almond flavoring, salt, and cup of whipped cream. Pour into tall glasses, partly filled with ice cream. Top with whipped cream and dash of nutmeg. Serves 10.

Heart's Desire Punch

1¼ cups water	2 cups strong tea
2½ cups sugar	2 cups pineapple juice
1 cup lemon juice	2 cups cranberries and juice
2 cups orange juice	1 teaspoon vanilla

Boil water and sugar for 12 minutes, then add remaining ingredients. Just before serving, add 2 gallons of water or soda water. Chill thoroughly. Serves 50.

Wedding Punch

4 quarts boiling water	2 quarts lemon ice
½ cup tea leaves	1 cup orange slices
1 quart sweet cherries, pitted	1 cup lemon slices
½ cup mint leaves	sugar

Steep tea leaves for 5 minutes in boiling water. Strain. Sweeten slightly. Lay cherries in tea and sprinkle mint leaves around them. Let stand for several hours surrounded by ice. Pour into large punch bowl with block of ice. Add lemon ice. Garnish with orange and lemon slices. Serves 50.

Lemon is a good summer flavor for many dishes. Hot summer vegetables served in butter taste even better with a squeeze of lemon juice. Lemon brings out the flavor in fish, and also the flavor in melons. Black bean soup is incomplete without a bit of lemon juice, and with all fruit and vegetable juices, lemon juice brings out the hidden flavors. Extra flavor is added to summer drinks by making ice cubes of lemonade.

Lemon Curd

3 lemons	4 egg yolks
1 egg white	1 cup sugar
	½ cup butter

Grate lemon rind very fine. Squeeze lemons and strain the juice. Strain the egg white through a very fine sieve, then beat gently with egg yolks. Cook sugar, butter, lemon rind and juice in double boiler, stirring constantly, until sugar is dissolved. Pour a little of this mixture over the eggs, stir, and then add eggs to the sugar-butter mixture. Stir constantly and cook over low heat until thick, 6 or 7 minutes. Put aside to cool. Pour into glass jar, store in refrigerator. Soften before using if necessary. Spread on buttered toast.

Lemon Meringue Pie

¾ cup sugar
3 tablespoons cornstarch
⅛ teaspoon salt
1 cup boiling water

2 egg yolks, slightly beaten
⅓ cup lemon juice
1 teaspoon butter
meringue

1 7-inch baked pie shell

Mix sugar, cornstarch, and salt. Stir in the boiling water gradually. Pour mixture into a saucepan and stir until it thickens. Beat egg yolks slightly. Add lemon juice. Stir the mixture into the saucepan. Cook one minute. Remove from heat. Stir in the melted butter. Cool slightly. Pour into baked shell. Cover with meringue.

MERINGUE

2 egg whites   ⅛ teaspoon salt
3 tablespoons confectioners' sugar
(or 2 tablespoons fine granulated sugar)

Beat egg whites until peak forms when beater is lifted from bowl. Add salt and 1 tablespoon sugar. Beat. Continue until all sugar is used. Pile meringue lightly on lemon filling. Bake in slow oven (300°) 15-20 minutes or until delicately browned.

161

Coolidge Lemon Custard Pie

2 eggs, separated	4 teaspoons flour
1 lemon, juice and grated rind	1 teaspoon melted butter
1 cup sugar	1 cup milk
⅛ teaspoon salt	1 7-inch pastry shell

Beat egg yolks until thick and lemon colored. Add lemon juice and rind, sugar, salt, flour, butter, and milk. Fold in egg whites, beaten stiff. Pour into unbaked pastry shell (with edges fluted) and bake in hot oven (450°) 10 minutes; reduce heat to moderate (350°) and bake 20 minutes longer.

This was the favorite custard-pie recipe of the late President Coolidge.

As tomatoes ripen in large enough numbers, they'll be a wonderful addition to outdoor meals, carried along in any kind of container with ice in it. Corn will be ripening now, and the young corn will roast nicely in a bed of ashes and good red coals. Turn the husks back enough to get most of the silk out, butter the corn, tie the husks back in place, and then bury in ashes for a half hour. Both tomatoes and corn lend themselves to appetizing variations.

Tomato Cup

2 large tomatoes	1 teaspoon tarragon
½ teaspoon basil	salt and pepper
1 teaspoon chervil	2 tablespoons mayonnaise
1 teaspoon shallots	¼ cup bread cubes
1 teaspoon wine vinegar	

Remove top of tomato; discard. Scrape out pulp. Add to pulp: basil, chervil, shallots, tarragon, salt, and pepper. Combine bread cubes with mayonnaise and vinegar and add to pulp mixture. Refill tomato cup. Serves 2.

Broiled Tomatoes

Cut thick slices of tomatoes and sprinkle with salt and pepper. Brush with butter and broil. Tomatoes may also be dipped in melted butter and bread crumbs, and sautéed.

Scalloped Tomatoes

4 tablespoons butter	2 tablespoons sugar
1½ tablespoons minced onion	salt and pepper
4 cups tomatoes, peeled and diced	1 cup buttered bread crumbs

Sauté onions in part of butter. Add to tomatoes. Combine sugar, seasonings, and bread crumbs. In a greased 2-quart casserole, place layer of tomatoes, then alternate with layers of crumb mixture and tomatoes, ending with crumbs on top. Dot with butter. Bake 30 minutes in moderate (350°) oven. Serves 6.

Corn Relish

36 ears of corn	4 cups sugar
20 tomatoes	2 cups sifted flour
10 onions	½ cup salt
2 bunches celery	1 teaspoon paprika
2 red peppers	1 teaspoon turmeric
2 green peppers	1 teaspoon dry mustard
1 gallon vinegar	

Remove corn from cob and combine with diced tomatoes, onions, celery, peppers. Mix with half the vinegar. Combine sugar, flour,

163

and seasonings, and add remaining vinegar. Combine the two mixtures and stir until smooth. Pour into large kettle, bring to boiling point, and simmer for 40 minutes. Put into sterilized jars. Seal. Yield: 20 pints.

Steamed Corn Pudding

3 cups dried apples	1 teaspoon salt
3 cups corn meal	2 cups water

Cover apples in water and soak overnight. Combine corn meal, salt, apples, and 2 cups water. Stir until thick. Place mixture in cotton bag (leaving room for mixture to swell during cooking). Steam for 3 hours. Serve hot with meat dish. Serves 6.

Corn Chowder

½ cup salt pork, chopped	½ teaspoon salt
4 tablespoons onion, chopped	2 cups water
¼ cup celery, chopped	2 tablespoons flour
2 tablespoons green pepper, chopped	2 cups warm milk
	2 cups corn kernels
1 cup raw potatoes, peeled and diced	chopped parsley

Sauté salt pork. Then add to pan and sauté onions, celery, and green pepper. Add potatoes, salt, and water, and simmer until potatoes are done. Add flour, milk, and corn. Heat all ingredients thoroughly. Sprinkle with chopped parsley. Serves 6.

Chapter 9   END OF SUMMER

August 2–September 9

THE rainy spell you may be complaining about in August lasts longer than most people believe it should. And when this happens, you are sure to be reminded that it rained on July 15 last, the day of St. Swithin. The superstition is that if it rains on this day, it will rain for forty days and then some. When St. Swithin died, he asked that he not be buried inside the cathedral where he had preached. Rather, he preferred being somewhere outside, perhaps along a walk, so he could be nearer to the people of his parish. But his instructions were not followed out. He was buried within. Several centuries later, when it was decided that his wishes should have been complied with, his remains were removed to a grave outside by a walk beneath the cathedral eaves. On the day of his reburial, legend says, it rained furiously and kept on for weeks and weeks. Thus his connection with heavy rains almost any time from July 15 and on into August.

Such rains will create a good deal of controversy among farmers and summer visitors. If there is one thing farmers do not like and cannot abide ("all signs fail in time of drought"), it is a drought. On the other hand, for the family at the seashore or on mountain, lake or river, a long spell of rain becomes almost unbearable. New England at this time of year—the days gradually shortening, the ground soon beginning to give up some of its accumulated best—can be cussed enough to bring on either a drought or a rainy spell. She has even been known to oblige with a little of each.

As August gets on a bit, however, there will be corn and tomatoes, beans, swiss chard, spinach, summer squash, young potatoes, and all sorts of wonderful fresh vegetables in the back-yard garden.

The worst of it is, of course, that when these vegetables do start showing up there is always an oversupply. Can or freeze, we say, and this rainy spell in August is just the time to do it.

On the calendar just now we are about opposite February. We think of February as a steadier month, one of winter, and do not notice too much the signs of spring in either its weather or its trees. And even if we tried to notice these internal changes during the month, it is doubtful, so invisible is their nature, that we would see them.

August is something like February in this respect. To most people, it is just the last full blooming of summer—

gorgeous days for swimming, boating, camping, hiking, or whatever outdoor pleasures are at hand. Yet if we look carefully, we will see here and there a yellow or red leaf dropping to the ground or some thicket which has completely turned.

What causes the color? Not frost alone certainly, because some leaves change before any frost has come. Drought perhaps? No, because the birch in that thicket, now fully turned, had a little stream near its roots. The chemical process that makes the color change is known, but what causes the process is as much a mystery as is the rising of the maple sap at the end of winter.

Then, too, you will notice there are not as many birds around. The swallows, for instance, depart some years as early as the sixth of August. It doesn't seem as if these birds stayed with us any too long—in about April or May, and off again in August. But remember they have a long way to go, some of them to South America, and they are taking no chances with storms at sea on these long flights.

Often neighbors complain that there "aren't too many birds around this year." Setting up our feeding stations earlier, instead of waiting until late in fall, might persuade many more to linger on.

The Dog Days which began on July 25 will run on through to the fifth of September. The rising and setting of the Dog Star Sirius is supposed (or was supposed in Roman times) to set these dates. Traditionally, we keep them pretty much as then, even though a calculation now of the rise and set of Sirius would change the date considerably. The rate of "precession" is about 50⅛ seconds per year, so that Sirius

167

has fallen back by now to just about one month earlier than in Roman times. As the Roman climate is no match for that of New England, it would not seem to matter too much anyway.

There is another "weather opposite" here in the saying, "As the days begin to shorten the heat begins to scorch them." You will remember the February one of, "As the days lengthen, the cold strengthens."

Another sign that August is fast preparing for something else is the amount of pollen which starts coming into the air about August 11. Hay-fever sufferers will not need to be told when it is around. We have seen the afflicted put to sea immediately, but we have seen too how even that has not been of any help. The mountains in the northern part of New Hampshire seem to afford the greatest relief.

There are many other complaints in August, too, from natives as well as visitors who have run up against poison oak or poison ivy—and even some eczema sufferers who are affected when the pollen from birch trees is on the loose. Another danger is in the hornet's nest or that of ground bees. Both dislike intrusion, and the latter are really dangerous to some people. Fortunately, those they affect in any serious way are generally aware of this, and when they walk where these bees may be, have an antidote along for immediate use.

Hard to explain—all these poisons and pollens—when at this season all seems lush and ready for man's harvesting. But surely they are all of a pattern.

Near August's end the fall fruits arrive. The famous Concord grape, you know, actually was perfected in Concord,

Massachusetts, and by now there is scarcely a New England farm which does not have an arbor of these, wild or otherwise, somewhere on the place.

A plum tree has quite a reputation as a weather forecaster. The saying goes—"a good plum year means a heavy winter" —and by and large we have found this quite true. There is a reason for this—one which of course will apply to all other fruit trees, too. Nature in bringing forth bountiful fruits in the fall is providing for those who must—especially birds and animals—withstand the winter ahead. Thus, the more plums—the harder the winter.

* * *

In another sense, *the more plums, the easier the winter.* That is, the more plums and fruits of every kind, the easier any winter will seem because of the enjoyment of fruit juices and jellies, jams and preserves. Those of us who grow or gather or crudely purchase fruit for preserving know that the hours of labor in late summer are more than paid for by hours of pleasure all winter.

If you planned to can only two jellies and preserves, you wouldn't go wrong with Concord grapes and beach plum. Jelly made from the dusky Concords holds all the delectable flavor of a ripe grape picked on a dewy summer dawn, and squeezed from its skin right into the mouth. Beach plum jelly has a literally heaven-sent flavor: according to an Indian legend, the Great Spirit clothed it in a tough skin so that the birds would have to leave us one kind of fruit. Fact is, the birds never touch beach plums!

Apple Jelly

Wash apples, remove stems, and cut in quarters. Place in large kettle and add water until almost covered. Cover kettle and cook fruit over low flame for about 20 minutes, or until apples are soft. Strain through several thicknesses of cheesecloth (do not squeeze). Measure juice. Boil for 5 minutes. Add ¾ cup sugar for each cup of juice. Continue boiling until jelly "sheets" from the spoon (220°). Pour at once into sterilized glasses. Seal with paraffin.

Beach Plum Jelly

Follow recipe for Apple Jelly, using one cup of sugar for each cup of juice.

Plum Butter

5 pounds plums
water
honey

Wash fruit. Put in kettle and cover with water. Cook until tender. Put through sieve to remove skin and pits. Measure plum pulp and add one half cup of honey for each cup of pulp. Mix well. Cook until thick over low flame. Seal in hot, sterilized jars.

How did Concord, Massachusetts, happen to associate its name with grapes? Well, there just weren't any good grapes thereabouts in 1836 when a Bostonian named Ephraim Wales Bull bought a house on Lexington Road near Hawthorne's "Wayside Inn." He went to work to breed a good sturdy grapevine that would stand up under the rigors of the climate.

Finding on his property a little vine that bore grapes of good flavor, he cultivated it for six years. The fame of his vines spread, nurserymen came to him for slips, and eventually his Concord grape became the most famous and sought after in the entire country. Many people became wealthy from their Concord grape vineyards, many from selling the grape juice, but Mr. Bull gained more fame than money. Death took him to Concord's Sleepy Hollow Cemetery under a stone that says: "He sowed—others reaped."

Concord Grape Jelly

Wash underripe grapes and remove stems. Place in kettle with a half cup of water for each four cupfuls of grapes. Boil the grapes until soft, then strain through cheesecloth or a jelly bag. Allow one cup of sugar for each cup of juice. Follow recipe for Apple Jelly (see page 170).

Concord Grape Wine

10 pounds grapes   3 quarts boiling water
5 cups sugar

Stem grapes, crush in stone jar. Add boiling water. Cover the jar and permit to stand for 3 days, stirring occasionally. Strain fruit in cheesecloth bag, and return juice to jar or crock. Add the sugar, cover the jar, and let stand until fermentation has stopped. Remove the scum, strain the juice, and bottle tightly.

Elderberry Wine

Follow above recipe, substituting elderberries.

Blackberry Wine

Follow above recipe, substituting blackberries.

Currant Jelly

Wash currants, place in kettle, allowing one fourth as much water as there is fruit. Cook over low flame until soft. Drain through cheesecloth. Allow one cup of sugar for each cup of juice. Follow recipe for Apple Jelly (see page 170).

Currant Catsup

5 pounds currants	1½ teaspoons cinnamon
3 pounds sugar	1 teaspoon salt
1 cup vinegar	1½ teaspoons allspice
1 teaspoon cloves	½ teaspoon pepper

Mix ingredients and boil slowly for about 2 hours, or until mixture is thick. Bottle. Yield: 2 quarts.

Quince Jelly

Wash quinces, cut into quarters, and remove seeds. Follow recipe for Apple Jelly (see page 170).

Quince Wine

quinces   white sugar

Grate very ripe quinces and strain through a muslin bag, then through a flannel bag. Add four pounds of white sugar for every gallon of juice. Stir well. Let stand in jugs or kegs. As it froths over, continue to refill from another jug. When it is quiet, bottle it. It can be used immediately, but if it is kept undisturbed for a year or two, it has a sparkling champagne quality.

Carrot Jam

5 pounds carrots   6 cups sugar

juice of 5 lemons

Pare and grate the carrots, add sugar and lemon juice. Cook slowly until mixture thickens.

Rose Petal Jam

Select rose petals carefully, using the most fragrant. Wash gently. Drain. For each cup of petals, measure one cup of sugar, add one teaspoon lemon juice, and a small quantity of water to dissolve the sugar. Combine sugar mixture with petals, and allow to stand for 3 hours, or until melted. Then cook over medium flame until the mixture thickens, about 30 minutes. Stir frequently.

A sprig of mint or a rose geranium leaf gives an interesting flavor to jellies. Simply place the leaf in the jelly jar before pouring in the hot liquid.

All Yankees will preserve enthusiastically for the winter, but they will show equal enthusiasm for eating as much fruit as possible in its pristine state.

Baked Pears

6 pears, pared	cinnamon
sugar	butter
	6 tablespoons water

Cut pears in half and core. Place in baking dish. Sprinkle with sugar and cinnamon. Dot with butter. Put water in bottom of dish, cover closely, and cook in slow oven (300°) for 1½ hours, or until tender.

Stewed Pears

2 cups water	6 pears, pared
1 cup sugar	2 teaspoons cinnamon
⅛ teaspoon salt	4 lemon slices

Boil water, sugar, and salt for 3 minutes. Add pears, cut in quarters, cinnamon, and lemon. Cook slowly until tender.

Deep-Dish Pear Pie

6 cups pears, sliced	½ teaspoon cinnamon
3 tablespoons lemon juice	¼ teaspoon nutmeg
½ cup sugar	butter
2 tablespoons flour	pastry crust

Sprinkle pears with lemon juice. Sift sugar, flour, cinnamon, and nutmeg. Mix with pears. Place mixture in buttered oven-proof dish. Dot with butter. Cover pie with pastry crust. Bake in hot oven (425°) for 30 minutes, or until pears are tender.

Peach Soufflé

2 cups peach pulp	½ cup sugar
2 tablespoons lemon juice	8 eggs, separated
¼ teaspoon salt	

Mash peeled ripe peaches until 2 cups of pulp are acquired. Then add lemon juice, sugar, beaten egg yolks, and salt. Fold in stiffly beaten egg whites and place in oven-proof dish. Bake in moderate oven (350°) for 40 minutes. Serve hot with cream or ice cream. Serves 4.

Peach Sauce

¼ cup butter	2 eggs, beaten
1 cup sugar	1 cup sliced peaches
1 cup milk, scalded	

Cream butter and sugar, adding eggs and scalded milk gradually. Beat thoroughly. Fold in sliced peaches.

Cherries were a popular fruit in America way back in Colonial days, and now they are gaining a new popularity because of their unique flavor and their use in meat sauces, desserts, and drinks.

Cherry Soup

1 pound red cherries, pitted	¼ teaspoon cinnamon
½ cup sugar	¼ teaspoon salt
2 teaspoons cornstarch	½ cup orange juice

1 cup red wine

Chop cherries very fine and mix with sugar, cornstarch, cinnamon, and salt. Stir in chopped cherries and orange juice. Bring mixture to a boil, stirring constantly. Remove from heat and stir in wine. Serve hot or cold. Serves 6.

Cherries Jubilee

1½ cups cherries	2 tablespoons kirsch
¼ cup brandy	1 pint vanilla ice cream

Heat cherries thoroughly. Add brandy. Set the brandy on fire, and when it is out, add kirsch. Serve hot on ice cream. Serves 4.

Cherry Cordial

6 pounds cherries	white sugar
rum	water

Wash and remove stems from cherries. Put in gallon jar and cover with rum. Let stand for 3 weeks. Pour off the clear liquor and put aside. Mash the cherries, including the stones, and drain in a flannel bag. Add this to the first liquor. For every 2 quarts of cherry liquor, dissolve 1 pound of white sugar in ½ cup of water. Bring to a boil and mix with the liquor. Stir well. Bottle and let stand for at least a month before using.

Cherry Slump

2 cups cherries

⅔ cup sugar

½ cup water

1 teaspoon cinnamon

1 cup flour, sifted

2 teaspoons baking powder

¼ teaspoon salt

½ cup milk

Remove stems and pits from cherries. Combine cherries, sugar, water, cinnamon. Bring to a boil. Mix and sift flour, baking powder, and salt. Add milk gradually. Drop dough by spoonfuls into the boiling fruit mixture. Cook 15 minutes with cover on and 10 minutes with cover off. Serve with cream. Serves 4.

Stewed Cherries

4 cups cherries

1½ cups boiling water

1 cup sugar

Remove stems and pits from cherries. Drop into boiling water. When tender, add sugar and cook 2 minutes longer. Serves 4.

Fruit Compote

1 cup pears

1 cup peaches

1 cup apples

1 cup pineapple

1 cup oranges

1 cup grapefruit

2 tablespoons sugar

1 teaspoon lemon juice

2 tablespoons orange juice

2 tablespoons kirsch

1 cup strawberries

Cut up fruit. Then, tasting as you proceed, add sugar, lemon juice, orange juice, kirsch. Let fruit stand in cool place for two hours. When served, garnish with strawberries, unhulled. Serves 6.

Cold Fruit Soup

2 cups grape juice	2 cloves
¼ cup orange juice	2 pears
¼ cup lemon juice	2 peaches
½ cup sugar	3 plums
1 teaspoon cinnamon	1 cup cherries

Simmer fruit juices, sugar, and seasonings for about 10 minutes. Then add fruits which have been cooked and cut into small sections. Combine with one cup of juice from the cooked fruits. Let stand for 2 hours. Place in refrigerator. Serves 5.

In this late summer, we are living in a happy pattern with respect to our swimming, boating, and other outdoor sports —which automatically furnishes us with healthy outdoor appetites.

Nature seems adjusted to the situation, because now it is that she heaps her greatest bounty upon us, ripening all the summer vegetables and fruits even faster than we can use them. In this happy extremity, it behooves us to shorten the meat courses and enjoy glorious salads full of the green luscious things of autumn's harvest. Beyond that, we will recall all our knowledge of the means of preserving food: drying, smoking, salting, pickling, canning, and freezing. Our forebears used all of these methods, and all are still in use.

Canning and freezing account for 90 per cent of our preservation of food. Pickling has a real importance for many foods, but most particularly in the case of cucumbers, as earlier noted, and cabbage.

From Colonial days, cabbage has been one of our most prized vegetables because it could be kept a long time in a cold vegetable cellar, and, still better, could be pickled.

Sauerkraut

The more mature cabbage is preferable, and it is best to make sauerkraut in the colder weather. First, shred cabbage on a grater designed for the purpose.

You need an earthenware crock with a lid. Drop a layer of shredded cabbage in bottom of crock, and sprinkle liberally with salt. Add cabbage and salt alternately until crock is full. Add water almost to the top, so that it appears when cabbage is pressed. Put on lid and let stand in a cool place for several days. Watch to make sure water level is maintained, and use as needed.

Cabbage is most wonderful, as all vegetables are, right out of the soil, and simply cooked in simple dishes.

Boiled Cabbage

Cut cabbage into small wedges and cook covered in ½ inch boiling water for 10 minutes. A small sprig of fresh caraway leaves added to the water gives an interesting flavor. Serve with butter, salt, and pepper.

Cabbage Fruit Salad

3 cups grated cabbage
1 cup apples, sliced thin
1 cup peaches, sliced
½ cup grapes, seedless
1 cup melon, diced

2 tablespoons honey
1 cup sour cream
2 teaspoons freshly minced
   tarragon
salt and pepper

Prepare salad just before serving. Toss fruits and cabbage, adding honey, sour cream, and seasonings. Serves 6.

Coleslaw and Apples

1 cup shredded cabbage	1 cup sour cream
1 cup diced apples	1 teaspoon dill seed
¾ cup walnut meats	salt and pepper

Combine ingredients. Chill. Serves 6.

Hot Apple Slaw

3 cups cabbage, shredded	2½ tablespoons butter
3 tablespoons vinegar	2 teaspoons minced tarragon
1 tablespoon sugar	2 medium-sized apples, grated

salt and pepper

Wash cabbage and put into stewpan with just the water that clings to leaves. Add vinegar, sugar, butter, and seasonings. Bring to a boil, then stir in apples. Reheat and serve. Serves 5.

Apple-Nut Coleslaw

1 cup cabbage, shredded	½ cup walnuts
1 cup apples, diced	½ cup mayonnaise

Combine cabbage and apples. Stir in nuts and mayonnaise. Serves 5.

Pineapple Slaw

3 cups cabbage, shredded	¼ cup vinegar
¼ cup green pepper, chopped	1 teaspoon salt
1 cup unpeeled apple, diced	lettuce
1 tablespoon sugar	1 cup carrots, shredded

6 slices pineapple

Combine cabbage with green pepper, apple, sugar, vinegar, and salt. Line salad bowl with lettuce and other greens. Top with carrots and pineapple. Serves 6.

We can note a preview of our frozen-food industry in this ancient recipe for keeping fruit fresh beyond its season; while the fruit isn't actually frozen, the same principle is applied of a low and constant temperature and exclusion of air.

"To preserve plumbs and cherries, six months or a year, retaining all that bloom and agreeable flavor, during the whole of that period of which they are possessed when taken from the tree.

"Take any quantity of plumbs or cherries a little before they are fully ripe, with the stems on: take them directly from the tree, when perfectly dry, and with greatest care so that they are not in the least bruised—put them with great care into a large stone jug, which must be dry, fill it full, and immediately make it proof against air and water, then sink it in the bottom of a living spring of water, there let it remain for a year if you like, and when opened they will exhibit every beauty and charm, both as to the appearance and taste, as when taken from the tree."

The modern deep-freeze has nothing new about it except the industry's ability to produce an inexpensive freezing unit. Our country forebears from time immemorial have gotten all their fruit and other pie fillings ready for use as soon as the thermometer went well below freezing. Then enough pies for the whole winter were made and put outdoors. Once frozen hard, they were stacked away in the icehouse or some other structure where the temperature could be expected to remain below freezing. Meat was preserved in the same way. The earliest method of all of preserving fruits and vegetables was, of course, dehydration. Neanderthal ancestors prowling hungrily in the antediluvian forests discovered fruits that had dried out in the sun but still under the circumstances deserved serious consideration. Several eons later a *homo sapiens* egghead suddenly contemplated the possibility of restoring the evaporated water. From then on, men deliberately dried fruits and vegetables during the lush season and undried them during the lean seasons.

New Englanders have used the process of dehydration from the first, usually glamorizing the job as an apple-paring and corn-husking party.

Boys and girls gathered at a big barn as though for a dance. Boys took shares of the green corn for husking, while girls divided the apples for paring.

Naturally, a good deal of mild flirtation took place. In the nature of things, the boys vied to see who was the better husker, and the girls tried to look piquant while peeling apples for dear life. When a girl was skillful enough to keep the peel of an apple all in one piece, she might throw it over her shoulder, and the boy quick enough to catch it collected a kiss for his trouble. One supposes that there was considerable collusion.

As the girls cored and quartered the apples, they tossed the pieces into buckets of cold water. When not an apple remained, the pieces would be strung with a darning needle into long ropes of fruit. These were hung near the kitchen

181

stove or, like the corn, in the sun to dry. Once dry, they were put in bags and stored in the attic to be drawn upon as needed.

Many people ate the dried apples as they were, much like raisins, but most of the apples found their way into the oven and emerged in such interesting shapes as fried pies or dried apple cake.

Fried Pies

2 cups flour	½ cup milk
½ teaspoon salt	2 cups dried apples, cooked
1 teaspoon baking powder	½ teaspoon cinnamon
3 tablespoons butter	½ teaspoon nutmeg
1 egg, beaten	1 tablespoon sugar

Sift flour, salt, and baking powder. Cut in the butter. Add egg and milk. Roll thin and cut in 5-inch circles. In the center of each place ½ cup dried apples sprinkled with spices and sugar. (Applesauce or other fruit may be substituted for apples.) Fold over, wet the edges with milk, and seal with a fork. Fry in hot fat until golden brown. Drain. Serve warm with cream. Makes 4 pies.

Dried Apple Cake

3 cups dried apples	2 cups nut meats
1 cup molasses	1 pound dates
1 cup butter	½ teaspoon salt
2 cups sugar	2 teaspoons soda
4 cups flour	2 teaspoons allspice
2 cups raisins	2 teaspoons nutmeg
1 teaspoon cinnamon	

Soak dried apples overnight in just enough water to cover. In the morning drain well and chop apples fine. Add molasses and simmer slowly until tender. Cool. Cream butter and sugar until light. Sift flour before measuring, sifting a little over the raisins, nut meats, and dates which have been chopped fine. Resift remainder of flour with salt, soda, and spices. Then stir the sifted ingredients into the butter mixture. Add other ingredients and when well blended stir in the apples. Bake in greased paper-lined loaf pans for about an hour at 350°.

Pure sunshine! Would you like to eat it or drink it? Have some honey, because in terms of color and flavor it is the nearest thing to sunshine of all our natural products! Honey is glorifying, poured over breakfast foods or dinner desserts, mixed with orange juice to make sauces for vegetables, or blended deliciously into desserts as a flavoring or syrup.

Honey should not be overlooked by a book such as this just because it is not a seasonal product. There are those who believe it confers beauty and longevity; that it gives energy and health, we know. Recipes? Use your own judgment in serving it on anything. Chances are it will add flavor and enjoyment. In many recipes throughout this book, it is used as the essential flavoring ingredient.

It will be seen as we near the end of this book how the New England cycle of weather has brought us around again to the season in which we started. We have been through all of the colors—the yellow of spring daffodils, the red of the roses, and the blue of the fall delphiniums. There is said to be a progression of these colors beginning with the yellow of early spring flowers, only to end again with the yellow of the goldenrod and the turned leaves of the beech and birch.

As to food, there is a similar natural cycle in terms of color and of flavor. Somehow, April cries out for maple syrup, May for the little wild strawberries, June for the earliest delicate vegetables, July for fish and shellfish, August for a bounty of tomatoes and corn, September and October for cranberries and apples—and, well, every month has its own harvest on land, sea, or in the air, and every month is joyously welcomed.

We have seen how the ground has taken in the cold of the atmosphere only to give it up to spring—and the warmth stored in it by spring and summer is lost before the first snows fly. We have watched the habits and movements of man, bird, and beast, as these climatic changes have taken place.

Yet what have we to hold—that will remind us—of all these seasons and the changes in them? Our memories, of course—the "I love you" flashing of Minot's Light across Massachusetts Bay, the lobster dinner at Pemaquid Point, the moonlight walk under the Harvest Moon. We are rich in these and many, many more.

We have picnicked on the beach and come home all of a sunburn. We have climbed the highest winter mountain and frozen toes and nose. But, as any New Englander will agree, there is nothing quite like New England food for the enjoying of New England weather.

FAVORITE RECIPES FROM NEW ENGLAND INNS

To the experienced traveler—is there any New Englander who isn't?—the ancient couplet

"Coil up your ropes and anchor here
Till better weather doth appear"

means, of course, the traditional *New England Inn* and its never failing success in being right on hand with just what "the doctor ordered" for weather fair or foul.

But to find refuge from stormy going is by no means the only reason you will seek out one of the very many inns of this region. All are rich in history, beauty, comfort, and hospitality—and their food is justly famed.

Through the courtesy of owners or managers, we are able to present here a favorite recipe from each of forty-one well-known New England inns.

THE LODGE AT SMUGGLER'S NOTCH
STOWE, VERMONT

Guivechi de Poisson à la Roumanie (Hors d'Oeuvres)

7 pounds fish: pike (carp, red mullet, codfish, whitefish, etc., may also be used, though the carp must be marinated beforehand)

½ pound carrots
1 turnip, small
½ pound string beans
½ pound green peppers
½ pound red peppers
2 onions
1 pound fresh green peas
10 ounces olive oil
1 ounce thyme

2 cloves
1 bay leaf
2 cloves garlic
1 bottle dry white wine
8 whole tomatoes
8 ounces fumet of fish or
    water
lemon juice
salt and pepper

Dice carrots, turnip, string beans, green peppers, red peppers, and onions; add a good handful of green peas. Mix these vegetables with olive oil, add a bouquet garni filled with thyme, cloves, bay leaf, and unpeeled garlic, and wet with wine, fresh tomato purée, fumet of fish or water. Add green peas at the last moment. Season with salt, pepper, and lemon juice. Cook 10 minutes. Place vegetables in earthenware dish, cover with the fish of your choice, add dry white wine, and bake in oven, always covered. The small fish are cooked whole; the larger fish are sliced in smaller sections. Before serving, add a few grains of Raisins de Corinthe Aigres. Serve cold. Serves 10.

COONAMESSETT INN
FALMOUTH, MASSACHUSETTS

Clam Chowder Base

1 quart quahogs	⅜ pound butter
1 cup water	¾ cup flour
1 pound onions	1 pint diced potatoes

Grind quahogs. Add water, and simmer for 5 minutes. Sauté onions in butter. Add flour. Cream for 5 minutes. Add diced potatoes which have been cooked separately in a small amount of water. Half milk and half cream should be added to an equal amount of the base for chowder.

BANGOR HOUSE, BANGOR, MAINE

Bangor House Fish Chowder

10 pounds fillet fresh haddock	6 quarts hot milk
2 pounds salt pork	2 teaspoons salt
6 medium-sized onions, finely diced	½ teaspoon pepper
	¼ pound butter
4 quarts raw diced Maine potatoes	

Fillet out fish, save bones for the broth. Make a broth by covering the bones and head of the fish with cold water, and let simmer for about an hour. Cut the fillet of haddock into 2-inch pieces. Cut the salt pork into ¼-inch cubes. Try out the fat. Add the onions; sauté until browned. Strain stock from the bones into the pork and onions, and let these simmer for 10 minutes. Boil the diced potatoes for 3 or 4 minutes, then drain. Pour the contents of the frying pan over the fish. Add the drained potatoes, cover, and cook 10 to 15 minutes. Then add the hot milk and salt and pepper. Bring to a boil. Just before serving, add butter, and let set for 5 minutes. Serves 50.

STONE BRIDGE INN, TIVERTON, RHODE ISLAND

Quahog Chowder

1 quart quahogs	¼ pound butter
6 potatoes, diced	1 quart light cream
2 chopped onions	salt and pepper

Open quahogs and save juice. Cover potatoes with water, and cook until tender. Sauté chopped onions in butter. Scald juice from quahogs. Add quahogs, onions, and scalded juice to potatoes, and bring to boiling point. Heat cream and add, with a tablespoon of butter. Salt and pepper to taste.

MIGIS LODGE, SOUTH CASCO, MAINE

Clam Stew with Sherry

2 quarts fresh Maine clams	1 pint good cream
1 quart water	1 bay leaf
4 ounces butter	salt, pepper, sherry, and
6 ounces flour	butter to taste
3 quarts milk	

Boil clams in water for 15 minutes. Strain through cheesecloth, and save liquor. After clams have cooled, pick over and chop. Make a roux with butter and flour. Add boiling liquor to roux, add chopped clams to mixture, then add hot milk and cream and extra butter. Season with salt, pepper, and sherry to taste. Makes 36 generous servings.

THE QUEEN ANNE INN
CHATHAM, MASSACHUSETTS

Lobster Bisque

1½-pound live lobster
1 quart water
1 cup condensed tomato soup
1 cup condensed cream of
    mushroom soup

1 cup cream of celery soup
4 tablespoons butter
salt and pepper
1 tablespoon minced
    pimento pepper

¾ cup sherry

Split live lobster; boil until shell is red. Cool lobster in broth. Remove lobster meat from shells. Discard shells, and mince lobster meat. Return lobster meat, liver, and coral (if any) to broth. Add condensed tomato soup, condensed cream of mushroom soup, and cream of celery soup. Season with butter, salt and pepper to taste, minced pimento pepper, and sherry wine. Lobster should be boiled in not more than 1 quart of water. This same liquid should make a proper consistency when combined with the 3 cups of condensed soups.

WHETSTONE INN, MARLBORO, VERMONT

Baked Halibut Whetstone

2 pounds halibut, cut in
    large, thick slices
butter
salt and pepper
milk

¼ pound mushroom pieces
    (fresh or canned)
1½ teaspoons BV or beef
    bouillon cubes
chives

Preheat oven to 400°. Place halibut in shallow, buttered, ovenproof dish. Dot with butter, sprinkle with salt and pepper. Pour milk around to almost cover the fish. Bake 20 minutes. Add

189

mushroom pieces. Dissolve BV in hot milk in dish, and stir and baste carefully. Bake 20 minutes more, until lightly browned. Add finely chopped chives and serve promptly. Serves 6.

WINDSOR HOUSE, WINDSOR, VERMONT

Fresh Lobster à la Newburg

14 ounces fresh cooked lobster
½ cup chopped pimento
4 tablespoons butter
¼ teaspoon nutmeg
dash of salt
3 tablespoons flour
4 cups half milk and half
    light cream

2 egg yolks
⅓ cup sherry
few drops Worcestershire
    sauce
dash of paprika
4 slices bread, toasted

Sauté lobster and pimento in butter; add nutmeg, salt, and flour; and sauté a few seconds. Add hot milk and cream, and let mixture come to a boil or until thickened. Stir in egg yolks, sherry, and Worcestershire sauce. Pour into casserole, and sprinkle with paprika. Serve piping hot, and decorate with toasted bread triangles. Serves 3 to 4.

THE WELD INN, WELD, MAINE

Escalloped Clams

1 egg
2 cups minced clams
    (including juice)
12 common crackers, rolled

1½ cups milk
¼ pound butter, melted
2 tablespoons sherry
dash of pepper

Beat egg in buttered dish. Add clams, crumbs, milk. Fold in

melted butter. Add sherry and pepper. Bake as you would a custard. Serves 4 generously.

BRANDON INN, BRANDON, VERMONT

Baked Stuffed Lobster, à la Thermidor

3 cooked 1½-pound lobsters	4 egg yolks
4 tablespoons butter	salt and pepper
1 cup fresh sliced mushrooms	Worcestershire sauce
paprika	Tabasco sauce
1 cup sherry	1 teaspoon prepared mustard
1½ cups heavy cream	Hollandaise sauce
	Parmesan cheese

Remove meat from lobsters, including claws, by cutting along each side of the back rather than from the inside. Cut into ½-inch slices, and sauté in butter with mushrooms. Paprika to color, and add sherry wine. When wine is almost cooked away, add cream, blended with well-beaten egg yolks, and pull away from heat. Add salt and pepper to taste, dash of Worcestershire, dash of Tabasco sauce, and prepared mustard. Stir gently until sauce is thickened. When desired consistency is reached, stuff back into lobster shell, top with Hollandaise sauce, Parmesan cheese, and bake in hot oven until golden. Serve on hot plate with gaufrette potatoes.

SHAWMUT INN, KENNEBUNKPORT, MAINE

Baked Stuffed Lobsters

2½-pound lobsters, boiled and cooled	12 tablespoons flour
	4 cups hot milk
8 tablespoons melted butter	1 cup American cheese, grated

Split lobsters through the middle. Remove meat and cut into

chunks. Place shells in pan, curling tails around. Blend flour slowly into butter over low heat. When thoroughly blended, slowly add hot milk. Cook 10 minutes, and let cool. Combine sauce with lobster chunks, and fill shells. Cover with cheese. Brown in a 425° oven. Serves 4.

TOLL HOUSE, WHITMAN, MASSACHUSETTS

Baked Stuffed Clams

1¼ cups chopped clams	2 tablespoons flour
or 1 can chopped clams	salt and pepper
3 tablespoons butter	4 clam or quahog shells
2 tablespoons chopped onion	buttered bread crumbs
dash of paprika	

Drain chopped clams and heat the juice. Melt butter, add onion, and cook until transparent. Add heated clam juice, cook and stir until thickened. Add chopped clams, and season with salt and pepper. Spoon into 4 large clam or quahog shells, and sprinkle with buttered bread crumbs. Shake paprika over the top, and place in 400° oven to heat through and brown. May be made ahead and heated at serving time. Serves 4.

YANKEE SILVERSMITH INN
WALLINGFORD, CONNECTICUT

Baked Stuffed Lobster in Casserole

5 ounces fresh boiled lobster	1 tablespoon Parmesan cheese
meat	touch of finely chopped garlic
½ cup fresh bread crumbs	1 ounce melted butter

Put lobster meat in a casserole. Cover with cheese and garlic.

Then cover this with bread crumbs and pour over it the melted butter. Bake at 400° about 7 minutes, or until golden brown. Serves 1.

DORSET INN, DORSET, VERMONT

Scalloped Oysters

½ pound butter, melted
3½ cups cracker crumbs, rolled
    (Boston baked butter
    crackers)

1½ cups water, using liquor
    of oysters
8 tablespoons Madeira wine
1 quart oysters

Mix melted butter with cracker crumbs. Add liquor and water and Madeira to oysters. Butter dish. Cover bottom with buttered crumbs, then layer (pint) of oysters, making 3 layers of crumbs and 2 layers of oysters. Salt to taste. Bake ¾ hour in moderate (375-400°) oven.

YANKEE PEDLAR INN
HOLYOKE, MASSACHUSETTS

Lobster Thermidor

1½-pound live lobster
½ teaspoon salt
butter
½ teaspoon paprika
1 ounce sherry

1 tablespoon cut mushrooms
1 tablespoon pimento
1 pint light cream
2 egg yolks
salt and pepper

Cheddar cheese

Boil lobster in salted water for 20 minutes. Remove lobster from water and split down center with sharp knife, belly side up. Remove small hard sack that lies just back of mouth opening.

Remove lobster meat from shell, and sauté gently in butter, adding paprika, sherry, cut mushrooms, and pimento cut in small pieces. In separate pan heat light cream, to which has been added the egg yolks, salt, and pepper. When mixture has thickened, add sautéed lobster meat with other ingredients. Place whole mixture in open lobster shell, and sprinkle generously with aged Cheddar cheese. Place in small flat pan, and heat in oven for 10 to 15 minutes.

PUBLICK HOUSE, STURBRIDGE, MASSACHUSETTS

Lobster Pie

FILLING, LOBSTER NEWBURG

4 tablespoons butter	2 tablespoons flour
½ cup sherry	1½ cups light cream
1 pound lobster meat,	salt and white pepper
coarsely chopped	2 egg yolks

A true Newburg is thickened only with egg yolks, but it is a tricky sauce to make and to keep from curdling, so a little flour is added in this recipe to stabilize the sauce. Melt 2 tablespoons butter in the top of a double boiler, add sherry and lobster meat. Let stand over simmering water while you make the sauce. Melt 2 tablespoons butter. Blend in flour, pour on 1 cup cream, and stir until the mixture comes to a boil. Season with salt and pepper. Beat egg yolks with a fork. Beat in ½ cup cream. Pour a little of the hot sauce over the yolks, stir, and blend the egg-cream mixture into the sauce. Stir until the sauce thickens, but do not let it boil. Add it to the lobster, blend lightly (stir lobster meat as little as possible to keep it from getting tough), and let stand over simmering water at least 10 minutes to blend the flavors. Remove from the fire. Put into 4 small individual casseroles or 1 larger one. Sprinkle with the following lobster pie topping. Bake for 15 to 20 minutes in a moderate oven at 350°, or brown immediately under the broiler. Serves 4.

LOBSTER PIE TOPPING

4 tablespoons butter
½ teaspoon paprika
½ cup cracker meal or finely crumbled stale white bread crumbs

2 tablespoons crushed potato chips
1 tablespoon grated Parmesan cheese
½ cup sherry

Melt butter with paprika, and let stand over a very low fire for about 5 minutes to cook the paprika a little. Blend with cracker meal or bread crumbs, crushed potato chips, Parmesan cheese, and sherry. No salt is needed; the potato chips will supply this.

THE OCEAN POINT INN
OCEAN POINT, MAINE

Yachtsman's Stew

½ pound salt pork, diced
2 pounds beef, cut in cubes
2 tablespoons flour
1 teaspoon salt
½ teaspoon pepper
1½ cloves garlic, minced
1 large onion, chopped

1 8-ounce can tomato sauce
1 bouillon cube, dissolved in 1 cup hot water
12 peppercorns
3 whole cloves
¼ cup chopped parsley
1 large bay leaf

¾ cup sherry or tart white wine

Sauté salt pork. Sprinkle beef with flour, salt, and pepper, and brown in pork fat. Add other ingredients except wine. Cover and simmer for 4 hours. After 3 hours add sherry or white wine.

Cook separately:

6 medium-sized potatoes   6 carrots
1 stalk celery, chopped

Cook vegetables until partially tender, then add to meat mixture for the last 15 minutes of cooking. The stew is thick and is served on dinner plate. Serves 8.

STONEHENGE, RIDGEFIELD, CONNECTICUT

Creamed Chicken Cannelloni au Gratin

CREAMED CHICKEN

1 whole chicken   salt and pepper
6 mushrooms   1 small glass sherry
butter   cream sauce

Boil chicken, mince. Mince and fry mushrooms in butter. Add chicken, salt and pepper to taste. Add sherry. Mix together in regularly prepared cream sauce.

HOLLANDAISE

3 egg yolks   salt
½ pound butter, melted   2 tablespoons cream sauce

Beat egg yolks over a hot fire until half cooked. Add melted butter and a pinch of salt, together with cream sauce to prevent curdling.

PANCAKES

1 egg   ½ cup flour
1 glass milk

Beat ingredients to a smooth batter and fry. Pour very small quantity in the pan and let it run until very thin.

196

Place creamed chicken in pancake and roll. Cover with Hollandaise. Sprinkle lightly with Parmesan cheese, and place under broiler for a few minutes, until brown.

THE RED BARN, WESTPORT, CONNECTICUT

Baked Individual Chicken Pot Pie, Red Barn Style

1½ ounces cooked white chicken meat

1½ ounces cooked dark chicken meat

1 tablespoon cooked green peas

1 tablespoon cooked diced young carrots

butter or chicken fat

flour

salt and pepper

chicken broth or stock

pie crust

Place cooked ingredients in individual casseroles. For each pie, cream 1 level tablespoon of butter or chicken fat with as much flour as will take up the grease in a frying pan. Add salt and pepper, and very gradually, while cooking, add chicken broth or stock until gravy is of desired consistency. It thickens further as it bakes. Top each casserole with pie pastry, and bake until pastry is brown.

WATERVILLE INN
WATERVILLE VALLEY, NEW HAMPSHIRE

Chicken Pie Supreme

2 cups chicken fat

1 quart flour

4 quarts hot chicken broth

3 quarts scalded milk

1 tablespoon salt

1 teaspoon Accent

egg coloring

6 quarts cooked chicken, diced

5 pounds frozen peas and carrots, cooked

Make a roux of chicken fat and flour. Cook 20 minutes, stirring occasionally, then add chicken broth and milk; beat until smooth.

Add salt, Accent, and egg coloring—just enough to make a nice yellow. Add chicken and precooked peas and carrots. This dish may be baked with a crust or served on biscuits. Serves 50.

THE DUBLIN INN
DUBLIN, NEW HAMPSHIRE

Dublin Inn Chipolata with Marron Purée

butter	button or sliced mushrooms
diced cooked ham	(precooked)
small pearl onions	small pitted olives
cooked and diced link sausages	brown cream sauce

large pieces of diced cooked chicken or turkey

Melt large lump of butter in heavy frying pan, add ham, onions, sausages, mushrooms, olives. Brown these ingredients lightly. Have ready a brown cream sauce (made by first browning flour and butter, instead of plain white sauce) in a double boiler. Add chicken or turkey, then browned ingredients. Stir lightly, heat, and serve with:

MARRON PURÉE

Place whipped sweet potatoes in a double boiler. Add finely chopped marrons, small amount of syrup from marron jar, lump of butter. Heat, stirring lightly.

THE RED LION INN
STOCKBRIDGE MASSACHUSETTS

Baked Stuffed Pork Chops with Sauce Sauterne

Use rib pork chops 1¼- to 1½-inch thick. Cut a pocket from the meaty portion through to the rib bone. Stuff with cranberry stuffing. Brown chops on both sides on a hot grill. Place in roast pan, cover with Sauce Sauterne, and bake (with pan covered) in a 400° oven for 30 to 35 minutes.

CRANBERRY STUFFING FOR 12 TO 15 CHOPS:

1 cup chopped onions	3 cups bread crumbs
2 cups celery, chopped	1 teaspoon poultry seasoning
1½ cups whole cranberries	1 tablespoon sugar
½ cup butter	salt and pepper

Sauté onions, celery, and cranberries for a few minutes in butter, then combine with other ingredients. Season with salt and pepper.

SAUCE SAUTERNE FOR 12 TO 15 CHOPS:

1 pint chicken stock	1 pint beef stock
1 pint sauterne wine	

THE TAVERN, GRAFTON, VERMONT

Beef Ragout en Casserole, Tavern Style

2 pounds top round beef	2 cups stock
salt and pepper	1½ cups dry red wine, heated
parsley	1 cup small onions, thinly
celery tops	sliced
¼ teaspoon thyme	1 cup fresh mushrooms, sliced
2 bay leaves	1 clove garlic, finely minced
2 tablespoons butter	1 cup freshly cooked diced
2 tablespoons flour	carrot

Cut beef into 1-inch squares, sprinkle freely with salt and pepper, place in deep saucepan, and let stand for 2 hours in cool place. Add cool water to cover, and push into center a bouquet garni consisting of sprigs of parsley, celery tops, thyme, and bay leaves tied in cheesecloth bag. Bring slowly to a boil, skim off scum, and gently simmer for 2 hours. Drain, remove stock, and keep stock hot.

Heat butter in heavy skillet, blend in flour, browning evenly, stirring constantly for 3 to 4 minutes. Slowly pour in 2 cups hot stock, stirring constantly until mixture boils. Add wine, onions, mushrooms, garlic, and meat cubes. Cover and simmer gently for 30 minutes. Halfway through simmering period add carrots. Serve piping hot in individual casseroles. Serves 10.

INDIAN CAVE LODGE
SUNAPEE, NEW HAMPSHIRE

Continental Beef Stew

1 clove garlic
⅓ cup shortening
3 pounds stewing beef, cubed
1 large onion, sliced
flour
salt and pepper
1 cup tomato sauce
½ cup beef broth
½ cup burgundy wine

⅓ cup sugar
herbs (bay leaf, orégano,
   sweet basil, thyme,
   rosemary, parsley)
½ pound fresh mushrooms
sliced green pepper
½ cup peas
4 potatoes, quartered
6 carrots, cut in 1-inch lengths

3 stalks celery, diced

Using a large heavy skillet, brown garlic in shortening. Add beef and onion. Dredge with flour, salt, pepper. Brown thoroughly. Then add tomato sauce, beef broth, burgundy wine, and sugar. Sprinkle herbs over this. Stir ingredients together and allow to simmer over low heat for 2 hours. Add fresh vegetables and cook an additional hour. If sauce thickens toward end of cooking period, add a few more ounces of wine to heighten flavor. Serves 8 to 10.

OLD RIVERTON INN
RIVERTON, CONNECTICUT

Baked Breast of Chicken à la Riverton

8 single chicken breasts	½ can mushrooms
salt and pepper	6 or 8 cubes ham
flour	cream sauce

Remove skin from chicken breasts and wash. Then sprinkle with salt and pepper, and roll in flour—very lightly. Place, rib side up, in a baking pan with a little water. Bake in oven for 30 minutes. Remove from oven, and add mushrooms and cubes of ham for flavor. Cover chicken breasts with cream sauce made with chicken stock. Return to oven and bake slowly in moderate oven, 350°, for about 1¼ hours, or until tender. Serves 8.

LIGHTED CHRISTMAS TREES INN
MARLOW, NEW HAMPSHIRE

Baked Beans

pea beans	salt
onions	black molasses
salt pork, diced	ginger
2 cloves garlic	dry mustard
ham bone	vinegar

Soak beans overnight. Next morning parboil until soft, along with a generous amount of onion, diced salt pork, 2 cloves garlic, and ham bone (good if some meat is still on it). Salt to taste. Put in bean pot with enough real black molasses to make it dark (some like brown sugar as well) and a pinch of ginger, dry mustard, dash of vinegar. Leave in oven with anything else baking (except cake), for the longer beans are baked, the better they are. They are best the second day's baking.

THE DOG TEAM TAVERN
MIDDLEBURY, VERMONT

French Dressing

4 cloves of garlic	1 tablespoon basil
1 cup sugar	1 tablespoon marjoram
⅓ cup dry mustard	1½ cups salad oil
⅓ cup salt (scant)	1½ cups vinegar

Mash garlic and rub well into dry ingredients. Add oil and vinegar.

THE GENERAL WOLFE INN
WOLFEBORO, NEW HAMPSHIRE

Roquefort Cheese Dressing

½ pound Roquefort cheese	½ cup sour cream
1 cup mayonnaise	juice of whole lemon

1 small grated onion

Mix all in blender. May be stored in refrigerator indefinitely.

CHRISTMAS FARM INN
JACKSON, NEW HAMPSHIRE

Chocolate Nut Cookies

1 package (6 ounces) chocolate tidbits	½ cup granulated sugar
	½ cup chopped nut meats
½ square bitter chocolate	½ teaspoon vanilla
2 egg whites	good pinch salt

Melt chocolate tidbits and bitter chocolate. Beat egg whites until stiff. Add gradually sugar, chopped nut meats, vanilla, salt, and melted chocolate. Drop by teaspoonfuls on ungreased pan covered with brown paper. Bake at 350° for 10 minutes. Cool before removing from paper.

THE RAGAMONT INN
SALISBURY, CONNECTICUT

Easy Popover Recipe

1 cup milk	½ teaspoon salt
1 cup sifted flour	2 eggs, beaten

Mix ingredients together. Grease muffin tins thoroughly. Place in cold oven. Set at 400°. Leave 30 minutes. Turn off heat. If not brown enough, leave another 10 minutes.

THE LORD JEFFERY
AMHERST, MASSACHUSETTS

Joe Froggers

7 cups sifted flour	¾ cup water
1 tablespoon salt	¼ cup rum
1 tablespoon ginger	2 teaspoons baking soda
1 teaspoon cloves	2 cups dark molasses
1 teaspoon nutmeg	1 cup shortening
½ teaspoon allspice	2 cups sugar

Sift together flour, salt, ginger, cloves, nutmeg, and allspice. Combine water and rum. Add baking soda to molasses. Thoroughly cream shortening and sugar. Add to shortening mixture half the dry ingredients, half the water and rum, then half the molasses, blending well after each addition. Repeat. Chill dough for several hours or overnight. Roll ¼-inch thick and cut with a 4-inch cutter. Bake on a greased cookie sheet in a moderate oven at 375° for 10 to 12 minutes, until lightly browned; watch carefully that they do not burn. Let stand a few minutes, then remove. Makes about 2 dozen cookies.

THE OLD MEETING HOUSE INN
LITTLE COMPTON, RHODE ISLAND

Butterscotch Sauce

1 cup sugar	¼ cup butter
1 cup dark corn syrup	pinch of salt

1 cup boiling water

Combine ingredients and boil to 285° on candy thermometer, stirring occasionally. Remove from heat, let cool about 3 minutes, then *slowly* stir in 1 cup boiling water, taking care not to scald hand in suddenly generated steam. When cold, serve on ice cream or cake desserts, pancakes, or waffles. May be stored in a tightly capped container, in or out of refrigerator.

WHITNEY'S, JACKSON, NEW HAMPSHIRE

Fruit Squares

2 cups raisins	2 teaspoons soda
2 cups cold water	2 teaspoons cinnamon
1 cup chopped dates	½ teaspoon ground cloves
2 cups sugar	½ teaspoon ground nutmeg
4 cups flour	½ teaspoon salt

1 cup chopped nut meats

Boil first 4 ingredients for a few minutes, and cool. Add remaining ingredients in order given. Mix thoroughly. Put in baking sheets 1-inch thick, and bake in a moderate oven, 350°. Cut in squares while hot.

WILLIAMS INN, WILLIAMSTOWN, MASSACHUSETTS

Blueberry Pudding

4 cups blueberries	½ cup water
1 cup sugar	8 thin slices white bread
	softened butter

This pudding is especially good when it is made with small ripe native blueberries rather than large cultivated ones. Bring the berries, sugar, and water slowly to a boil, and simmer for 10 minutes. Remove the crusts from the bread, and spread each slice with softened butter. If a small 9 x 4½-inch loaf pan is used, the bread will just fit, 2 pieces in each layer. Place the bread, buttered side down, in the pan, and cover with hot berries. Continue these layers, ending with berries. Let stand until cool, then chill in refrigerator. To serve, unmold on a platter, and slice. Serve with cream or ice cream. Serves 8 to 10.

COLBURN HOUSE
MANCHESTER CENTER, VERMONT

Pumpkin-Mince Pie

1 cup canned pumpkin	2 eggs, slightly beaten
½ cup brown sugar	14½ ounces evaporated milk
1 teaspoon pumpkin pie spice	2½ cups mincemeat
½ teaspoon salt	1 9-inch unbaked pie shell

Combine pumpkin, sugar, spice, salt, eggs, and milk, and beat until smooth. Spread mincemeat evenly over pie shell. Ladle pumpkin mixture carefully over mincemeat. Bake at 450° for 10 minutes, then at 350° for about 45 minutes, until filling is firm in center.

ANNISQUAM INN, ANNISQUAM, MASSACHUSETTS

Special Coffee Cake

CAKE BATTER

¼ cup butter or margarine
2 beaten eggs
1½ cups all-purpose flour,
    sifted

2 teaspoons baking powder
1 cup sugar
½ cup milk
pinch of salt

FILLING

2 tablespoons butter or
    margarine
1 cup chopped walnuts

1 cup brown sugar
2 tablespoons flour
1 tablespoon cinnamon

Prepare cake batter and set aside. Prepare the filling by melting butter and pouring over nuts, brown sugar, flour, and cinnamon. Then blend with finger tips. Pour half of the batter into 8 x 12-inch baking pan. Sprinkle half the nut mixture over it. Add remaining batter and top with remaining nut mixture. Bake in 375° oven for 30 minutes.

SILVERMINE TAVERN, NORWALK, CONNECTICUT

Honey Buns

4½ ounces sugar
2 egg yolks
1½ teaspoons salt
1 cup milk, warm
4½ ounces shortening
1½ ounces yeast

½ cup water, warm
1 teaspoon sugar
1½ pounds flour
melted butter
brown sugar
cinnamon

Combine sugar, egg yolks, and salt. Blend warm milk and shortening, and add to yolk mixture. Crumble yeast into warm water, add a teaspoon of sugar. Dissolve and let rise a little. Combine with egg mixture. Gradually add flour until dough is stiff. Place in a greased bowl, cover, and place in warm spot until dough doubles in bulk. Roll dough out oblong, and brush with melted butter. Sprinkle thickly with brown sugar and cinnamon. Roll up like a jelly roll, and cut in 1-inch slices. Place in buttered muffin pans, brown sugar and butter in bottom of pan. Let rise for about ¾ hour. Bake in moderate oven for 20 to 30 minutes until brown on bottom. Remove from pans as soon as taken from the oven. Makes about 3 dozen small buns.

TIP-TOP INN, SHREWSBURY, VERMONT

Pineapple Fritters with Chantilly Sauce

PINEAPPLE FRITTERS

2⅔ cups sifted flour	½ teaspoon salt
4 teaspoons baking powder	1⅓ cups milk
	2 eggs, well beaten
1 can crushed pineapple, drained (1-pound size)	

Mix and sift dry ingredients, add milk gradually, and eggs. Add drained pineapple to batter. Fry until light brown. Serve with Chantilly Sauce.

CHANTILLY SAUCE

4 egg yolks	1 teaspoon vanilla
1 cup sugar	2 tablespoons melted butter
1 teaspoon nutmeg	1 cup cream

Beat together all ingredients except the cream until very thick. Add cream, beaten stiff. Chill. Serves about 20.

SQUAW MOUNTAIN INN
MOOSEHEAD LAKE, MAINE

Blueberry Chiffon Pie

1½ pints fresh blueberries	4 ounces cornstarch
18 ounces sugar	1 pint egg whites
½ pint water	red coloring

6- or 10-inch baked pie shells

To fresh blueberries, add 8 ounces sugar and crush. Put on slow fire until they boil. Dissolve cornstarch in water and add to blueberries to thicken. Put egg whites in beater, add 2 ounces sugar, then beat stiff. When stiff, add 8 ounces more sugar, and continue to beat until sugar is dissolved. Add hot thickened blueberries to mixture of sugar and egg whites, and fold in with spoon until cool enough to stand your hand. Then add and mix thoroughly a few drops of red color to make a rich blueberry color. Fill pie shells, and put in refrigerator. When cooled, add whipped cream and spread over top.

THE NORTHFIELD
EAST NORTHFIELD, MASSACHUSETTS

Strawberry Chiffon Pie

PIE SHELL

4 egg whites	¼ teaspoon cream of tartar

1 cup sugar

Beat egg whites until frothy; add cream of tartar; beat until stiff. Add sugar and continue to beat until stiff and glossy. Put in 9- or 10-inch pie tin. Bake in slow oven (280°) for 20 minutes, then increase heat to 300° and bake for 40 minutes.

FILLING

2 cups strawberries, hulled	¼ cup cold water
½ cup sugar	1 teaspoon lemon juice
1 tablespoon gelatine	red coloring

Add sugar to strawberries. (For frozen strawberries, use 1½ cups berries with ¼ cup sugar.) Mix gelatine in cold water, then dissolve by heating over hot water. Cool. Add lemon juice and drop of coloring. Add to berries. Cool until syrupy.

Line pie shell with thin layer of whipped cream. Pour in filling. Cover pie with thin layer of whipped cream. Let stand overnight or 24 hours.

WAYSIDE INN, SUDBURY, MASSACHUSETTS

Wayside's Apple Indian Pudding

2 cups milk, scalded	½ cup molasses
½ cup corn meal	¼ cup sugar
1 pound apples, peeled, cored, and sliced	½ tablespoon salt
	1½ teaspoons butter
1 quart cold milk	

Stir corn meal in scalded milk and cook for 10 minutes, beating continually. Add apples, molasses, sugar, salt, and butter. Mix together, and add cold milk. Pour mixture into buttered baking dish. Bake for 2½ to 3 hours at 300°. Allow pudding to cool. Cold pudding will have a clear amber jelly throughout. Serve with heavy cream or ice cream. Serves 8 to 10.

Index

Anadama bread, 71-72
Angelica candy, 59-60
Angus toffee, 59
Apples
    baked, 38
    Christmas, 58
    cider, 41
    coleslaw and, 179
    dried, 182-183
    dumplings, 38-39
    and ham, 39
    Indian pudding, Wayside's (Wayside Inn, Sudbury, Mass.), 209
    jelly, 170
    nut coleslaw, 179
    pan dowdy, 38
    pie, 37
    and pork chops, 39
    and sausage, 39
    slaw, hot, 179
    stewed, 60-61
Applesauce, 40
    cake, 40
    cream, 40
Apricot-prune stuffing, 50
Aroostook savory supper, 30
Asparagus
    amandine, 129
    creamed, 128
    fresh boiled, 128
    au gratin, 128
    tips with ham, 129
Atholl brose, 65

Baked beans (Lighted Christmas Trees Inn, Marlow, N. H.), 201
Bananas, grilled for barbecue, 145
Barbecue recipes, 145-146
Beach plum jelly, 170
Beans, baked (Lighted Christmas Trees Inn, Marlow, N. H.), 201
    Boston baked, 26-27
Bear, roast, 48
Bear marinade, 48
Beef bacon, creamed, 25
Beef, dried, 25
Beef ragout en casserole, Tavern style (The Tavern, Grafton, Vt.), 199-200
Beef stew, continental (Indian Cave Lodge, Sunapee, N. H.), 200
Beets
    baked, 138
    baked in honey, 138

in cranberry sauce, 138
    Harvard, 138
Black and gold marble cake, 75
Black walnut cake, 77-78
Blackberry wine, 171
Blueberries
    bread-and-butter pudding, 156
    chiffon pie (Squaw Mountain Inn, Moosehead Lake, Me.), 208
    crisp, 156
    muffins, Maine, 155
    pancakes, 94-95
    pudding (Williams Inn, Williamstown, Mass.), 205
    slump, 154
    upside-down cake, 155
Boiled dinner, New England, 24-25
Boston baked beans, 26-27
Boston black bean soup, 22-23
Boston brown bread, 27-28
Boston cream pie, 82
Bread, 71-74
    Boston brown bread, 27-28
    hot cross buns, 99
    popovers, 203
Bread and butter pickles, 117
Brook trout, broiled, 108
Buckwheat cakes, 95
Butterscotch, old-fashioned, 59
Butterscotch sauce (The Old Meeting House Inn, Little Compton, R. I.), 204

Cabbage
    apple-nut coleslaw, 179
    boiled, 178
    coleslaw and apples, 179
    fruit salad, 178-179
    hot apple slaw, 179
    pineapple slaw, 179-180
    soup, Vermont, 21
Cakes
    applesauce, 40
    black and gold marble, 75
    black walnut, 77-78
    blueberry upside-down, 155

chocolate mint, 76
    coconut, 132-133
    cranberry roly-poly, 10-11
    cranberry shortcake, 10
    dried apple, 182-183
    Dundee, 54-55
    election, 78-79
    fruit squares (Whitney's, Jackson, N. H.), 204
    gingerbread, 81
    honey buns (Silvermine Tavern, Norwalk, Conn.), 206-207
    Maine molasses doughnuts, 81
    pound, 82
    scripture, 78
    special coffee (Annisquam Inn, Annisquam, Mass.), 206
    spiced doughnuts, 41
    strawberry sandwich, 134-135
    strawberry shortcake, 135
    uncooked fruit, 56-57
    Wellesley fudge cake, 77
Canapes, and herbs, 84
Candied sweet flag, 114
Candy
    angelica, 59-60
    Angus toffee, 59
    butterscotch, old-fashioned, 59
    honey scotch, 57
    horehound, 58
    popcorn balls, 58-59
Carrots
    boiled, 137
    and green peas, 137
    honey glazed, 137
    jam, 172
Catsup, currant, 172
Celery, stuffed with water cress and Roquefort, 115
Celery-bread stuffing, 50
Chantilly sauce (Tip-Top Inn, Shrewsbury, Vt.), 207
Cherries
    cordial, 175
    jubilee, 175
    slump, 176
    soup, 175
    stewed, 176
Chestnut stuffing, 49

Chicken
  baked breast of, à la Riverton (Old Riverton Inn, Riverton, Conn.), 201
  barbecued, 145
  creamed, cannelloni au gratin (Stonehenge, Ridgefield, Conn.), 196-197
  pie supreme (Waterville Inn, Waterville Valley, N. H.), 197-198
  pot pie, Red Barn style (The Red Barn, Westport, Conn.), 197
  smothered in oysters, 19
Chipolata with marron purée (The Dublin Inn, Dublin, N. H.), 198
Chocolate dream frosting, 75-76
Chocolate mint cake, 76
Chocolate nut cookies (Christmas Farm Inn, Jackson, N. H.), 202-203
Chowders
  clam, 147
  clam chowder base (Coonamessett Inn, Falmouth, Mass.), 187
  corn, 164
  Daniel Webster's fish chowder, 23
  fish, Bangor House (Bangor House, Bangor, Me.), 187-188
  kedgeree, Conn., 112
  Nantucket scallop chowder, 21
  quahog (Stone Bridge Inn, Tiverton, R. I.), 188
  Rhode Island quahog, 149
  vegetable, 22
  Yankee clam, 150
Christmas apples, 58
Cider, 41
  champagne, 41-42
  sauce, 101
Clambake directions, 147-149
Clams
  baked stuffed (Toll House, Whitman, Mass.), 192
  broth, 147-148
  chowder, 147
  chowder base (Coonamessett Inn, Falmouth, Mass.), 187

chowder, Yankee, 150
escalloped (The Weld Inn, Weld, Me.), 190-191
stew with sherry (Migis Lodge, South Casco, Me.), 188
Coconut cake, 132-133
Coconut ice cream, 131-132
Codfish balls, 27
Coffee cake, special (Annisquam Inn, Annisquam, Mass.), 206
Coffee frosted, 159
Coffee punch, 64
Coleslaw, see Cabbage and apples, 179
Compote, fruit, 176
Concord grape jelly, 171
Concord grape wine, 171
Connecticut kedgeree, 112
Cookies
  chocolate nut (Christmas Farm Inn, Jackson, N. H.), 202-203
  Joe Froggers (The Lord Jeffery, Amherst, Mass.), 203-204
  old-fashioned molasses, 79
Corn
  chowder, 164
  grilled, for barbecue, 146
  relish, 163-164
Corn meal mush, 29
Corn pudding, steamed, 164
Court bouillon, 153
Crabs
  deviled, 151-152
  meat mousse, 152
  soft-shell, sautéed, 152
Crackling bread, 72
Cranberries
  baked, 13
  ham slices, 12
  meringue pie, 11-12
  pie, 11
  pudding, steamed, 12
  roly-poly, 10-11
  sauce, 13
    beets in, 138
  shortcake, 10
  snowballs, 11
  stuffing, 61, 199
Creamed beef bacon, 25
Creamed chicken Cannelloni au gratin (Stonehenge, Ridgefield, Conn.), 196-197
Cucumber relish, raw, 116
Cucumber sauce, 116
Cucumbers with sour cream, 116

Currant jelly, 172
Currant catsup, 172
Custard, strawberry, 136

Dandelion salad, 113
Dandelion wine, 113
Deer loaf, 48, see also Venison
Doughnuts
  Maine molasses, 81
  spiced, 41
Dressings, see Stuffings, Salad dressings
Dried apple cake, 182-183
Dried beef, 25
Drinks, 63-65, 157-160
Dundee cake, 54-55

Eggnog, 63
  Harvard Club, 63
Eggs
  herbs and, 84
  in maple syrup, 96
  mussel omelette, 98
  sauce, 154
Elderberry blossom fritters, 95
Elderberry wine, 171
Election cake, 78-79

Fillet of sole, sautéed, 111
Fish, 83, 108-112; see also Codfish, Haddock, etc.
  baked, with almond sauce, 83
  baked halibut Whetstone (Whetstone Inn, Marlboro, Vt.), 189-190
  baked, with sour cream, 83
  broiled brook trout, 108
  codfish balls, 27
  Connecticut stuffed baked shad, 109-110
  Guivechi de poisson à la Roumanie (The Lodge at Smuggler's Notch, Stowe, Vt.), 186
  and herbs, 86
Fowl, turkey, roast, 48
French dressing (The Dog Team Tavern, Middlebury, Vt.), 202
Fried pies, 182
Frostings, 75-76
  chocolate dream, 75-76
  marshmallow, 132-133
  peppermint boiled frosting, 76
Frosting, Wellesley fudge cake, 77

Fruit, *see also* Apples, Peaches, etc.
apples, 37-42
blueberries, 154-156
cake, uncooked, 56-57
cherries, 175-176
compote, 176
grilled, for barbecue, 145-146
peaches, 174
pears, 173-174
raspberries, 156-157
rhubarb, 117-119
soup, cold, 176
squares (Whitney's, Jackson, N. H.), 204
strawberries, 134-136
and vegetable salad, 139
Fudge cake, Wellesley, 77

Game, 43-48
bear, 48
grouse, 44-45
and herbs, 86
pheasant, 45
quail, 45
rabbit, 46
venison, 46-48
wild duck, 43-44
Gingerbread, 81
Goose, roast, with apples, 60-61
Goose dressing, 61
Grapefruit and orange peel, 57
Green peas
carrots and, 137
and lettuce, 137
with mint, 137
Greens, 113-115
Grouse
broiled, 44-45
roast, 44
Guivechi de Poisson à la Roumanie (The Lodge at Smuggler's Notch, Stowe, Vt.), 186

Haddock
baked fillets of, 110-111
with oyster stuffing, baked, 111
Halibut, baked, Whetstone (Whetstone Inn, Marlboro, Vt.), 189-190
Ham
apples and, 39
with asparagus tips, 129
baked, 100
baked, and fruit, 100
cranberry ham slices, 12
oyster-ham sandwich, 19
Hasty pudding, 29

Haymakers' switchel, 158
Heart's desire punch, 159
Herb butter, 85
Herb teas, 85
Herbs, 84-87
Herring, marinated, 112
Hollandaise sauce, 197
Honey buns (Silvermine Tavern, Norwalk, Conn.), 206-207
Honey scotch, 57
Horehound candy, 58
Hot cross buns, 99

Ice cream
coconut, 131-132
cranberry snowballs, 11
peach, 130
rhubarb, 130
strawberry, 134
vanilla, 130
Iced tea and rum, 159
Indian pudding, baked, 80

Jellies and preserves, 170-173
conserve, 119
pumpkin, 17
Joe Froggers (cookies), (The Lord Jeffery, Amherst, Mass.), 203-204
Johnnycake, Rhode Island, 73

Kedgeree, Connecticut, 112

Lamb
chops, broiled, 103
leg of, 102
steak casserole, 102-103
stew, 103
tomato cups, cold, 104
Lemon curd, 160-161
Lemon custard pie, Coolidge, 162
Lemon meringue pie, 161
Lobster
baked, 150
baked stuffed (Shawmut Inn, Kennebunkport, Me.), 191-192
baked stuffed, in casserole (Yankee Silversmith Inn, Wallingford, Conn.), 192-193
baked stuffed, à la Thermidor (Brandon Inn, Brandon, Vt.), 191
bisque (The Queen Anne Inn, Chatham, Mass.), 189
boiled, 150

fried, 151
Newburg, 151
Newburg (Windsor House, Windsor, Vt.), 190
pie (Publick House, Sturbridge, Mass.), 194-195
Thermidor (Yankee Pedlar Inn, Holyoke, Mass.), 193-194

Mackerel, baked, 110
Maine molasses doughnuts, 81
Maple charlotte, 97
Maple mousse, 97
Maple raisin pudding, 96
Maple sauce, 97
Maple syrup, 94-97
eggs in, 96
Maple syrup pie, 95-96
Marble cake, black and gold, 75
Marinade
bear, 48
venison, 46
Marinated herring, 112
Marron purée, 198
Marshmallow frosting, 132-133
Mead, 64-65
Meat, *see* Beef, Ham, Lamb, Pork
boiled beef tongue, 26
frugal pie, 28
New England boiled dinner, 24-25
red flannel hash, 25
Yankee pot roast, 24
Meat pies, frugal pie, 28
Milk, spiced, 158
Mince-pumpkin pie, 205
Mincemeat, 62
Mincemeat pie, 63
Mocha punch, 159
Molasses
cookies, old-fashioned, 79
Maine molasses doughnuts, 81
pie, 80
popcorn balls, 58-59
Mussel omelette, 98
Mussels, sauce for, 98
Mustard sauce, 101

New England boiled dinner, 24-25

Onions, grilled, for barbecue, 146
Orange and grapefruit peel, 57
Orange sauce, 102
212

Oranges, grilled for barbecue, 145
Oysters
chicken smothered in, 19
cocktail sauce, 17
ham sandwich, 19
scalloped, 18, (Dorset Inn, Dorset, Vt.), 193
skewered, 18
stew, 18
stuffing, 111

Pancakes
blueberry, 94-95
buckwheat cakes, 95
potato, 94
Vermont thins, 94
Parker House rolls, 72-73
Peaches
grilled for barbecue, 146
ice cream, 130
sauce, 174
soufflé, 174
Pears
baked, 173
deep-dish pie, 174
grilled for barbecue, 145
stewed, 173
Pecan pie, 96
Peppermint boiled frosting, 76
Pheasant
broiled, 45
pan-broiled, 45
Pickles, see Relishes
Pies
apple, 37
Boston cream, 82
blueberry chiffon (Squaw Mountain Inn, Moosehead Lake, Me.), 208
Coolidge lemon custard, 162
cranberry, 11
cranberry meringue, 11-12
deep-dish pear, 174
fried, 182
frugal (meat pie), 28
lemon custard, Coolidge, 162
lemon meringue, 161
maple syrup, 95-96
mincemeat, 62-63
molasses, 80
pecan, 96
pumpkin, 17
pumpkin-mince (Colburn House, Manchester Center, Vt.), 205
rhubarb, 117-118

strawberry chiffon (The Northfield, East Northfield, Mass.), 208-209
Pimm's cup, 159
Pineapple
fritters with Chantilly sauce (Tip-Top Inn, Shrewsbury, Vt.), 207
grilled, for barbecue, 145
slaw, 179-180
Plum
butter, 170
pudding, 55
Governor Bradford's, 56
Pomander balls, 54
Popcorn balls, 58-59
Popovers (The Ragamont Inn, Salisbury, Conn.), 203
Pork
chops, apples and, 39
chops, baked stuffed, with Sauce Sauterne (The Red Lion Inn, Stockbridge, Mass.), 198-199
crown roast of, 61
Potatoes
Aroostook savory supper, 30
baked stuffed, 30-31
grilled, for barbecue, 146
mashed Mainers with mint, 30
new, in cream, 154
pancakes, 94
salad, cold, 32
salad, hot, 31
Pound cake, 82
Preserves and jellies, 17, 119, 170-173
Puddings
apple Indian (Wayside Inn, Sudbury, Mass.), 209
baked Indian, 80
blueberry (Williams Inn, Williamstown, Mass.), 205
blueberry bread-and-butter, 156
blueberry slump, 154-155
cherry slump, 176
corn, steamed, 164
cranberry steamed, 12
Governor Bradford's plum, 56
maple raisin, 96
plum pudding, 55
pumpkin chiffon, 16

rhubarb bread, 119
Yankee Christmas, 55
Wayside's apple Indian, 209
Pumpkin
chiffon pie, 16
chiffon tarts, 16
mince pie (Colburn House, Manchester Center, Vt.), 205
pie, 17
preserve, 17
seeds, toasted, 15
Punch, see Drinks

Quahog chowder (Stone Bridge Inn, Tiverton, R. I.), 188
Quahog chowder, Rhode Island, 149
Quail
broiled, 45
on skewers, 45
on toast, 45
Quince jelly, 172
Quince wine, 172

Rabbit
fried, 46
smothered, 46
stew, 46
Raisin bread, 74
Raisin sauce, 101
Raspberry
cooler, 157
cream, 156-157
float, 157
royal, 157-158
Red flannel hash, 25
Relishes
bread and butter pickles, 117
corn, 163-164
raw cucumber, 116
Rhode Island johnnycake, 73
Rhode Island quahog chowder, 149
Rhubarb
bread pudding, 119
ice cream, 130
pie, 117-118
raspberry-orange conserve, 119
roly-poly, 118
and strawberries, 134
and strawberry sauce, 119
tonic, 118
wine, 118
Roquefort cheese dressing (The General Wolfe Inn, Wolfeboro, N. H.), 202
Rose petal jam, 172

213

Rum
  Christmas punch, 64
  hot buttered, 64
  iced tea and, 159
  sauce for pudding, 56

Salad dressings
  French, 202
  Roquefort cheese, 202
Salads
  apple-nut coleslaw, 179
  cabbage fruit, 178-179
  cold potato, 32
  coleslaw and apples, 179
  dandelion, 113
  fruit and vegetables, 139
  and herbs, 86
  hot apple slaw, 179
  hot potato, 31
  pineapple slaw, 179-180
  trout, 109
Salmon, "boiled," 153
Sardines, 112
Sauces
  butterscotch (The Old
    Meeting House Inn,
    Little Compton, R. I.),
    204
  Chantilly (Tip-Top Inn,
    Shrewsbury, Vt.), 207
  cranberry, 13
  cucumber sauce (for
    fish), 116
  egg, 154
  for ham, 101-102
  hollandaise, 197
  for ice cream, 131
  maple sauce, 97
  for mussels, 98
  oyster cocktail, 17
  peach, 174
  raisin, 101
  rhubarb and strawberry,
    119
  rum (for pudding), 56
  Sauterne (The Red Lion
    Inn, Stockbridge,
    Mass.), 199
Sausage, apples and, 39
Scallions on toast, 115
Scallops
  Casino, 20
  chowder, Nantucket, 21
  vinaigrette, 20
  in wine, 20
Scripture cake, 78
Scrod, broiled, 110
Shad, stuffed baked, Con-
  necticut, 109-110
Shellfish
  crab, 151-152
  lobster, 150-151
Sherry cobbler, 158
Smelts
  baked, 112

  broiled, 112
  sautéed, 112
Sole, fillets of, sautéed,
  111
Sorrel soup, 115
Soups, 21-23; see also
  Chowders
  Boston black bean, 22-
    23
  cherry, 175
  cold fruit, 177
  sorrel, 115
  split pea, 22
  stockpot, 21-22
  Vermont cabbage, 21
Split pea soup, 22
Squash
  acorn, stuffed, 15
  Hubbard, baked, 14
  pie, 15
  seeds, toasted, 15
Stews
  clam, with sherry (Migis
    Lodge, South Casco,
    Me.), 188
  continental beef (Indian
    Cave Lodge, Sunapee,
    N. H.), 200
  lamb, 103
  oyster, 18
  yachtsman's (The Ocean
    Point Inn, Ocean
    Point, Me.), 195-196
Strawberries
  chiffon pie (The North-
    field, East Northfield,
    Mass.), 208-209
  custard, 136
  dipped, 135-136
  ice cream, 134
  preserves, 136
  and rhubarb, 134
  and rhubarb sauce, 119
  sandwich, 134-135
  shortcake, 135
Stuffings
  cranberry, 61, 199
  goose dressing, 61
  oyster stuffing, 111
  turkey, 49-50
Sweet flag, candied, 114
Sweet potatoes, grilled for
  barbecue, 146
Switchel, haymakers', 158
Syllabub, 65

Tomatoes
  broiled, 163
  cup, 162-163
  grilled for barbecue, 146
  lamp cups, cold, 104
  scalloped, 163
Trout, broiled brook, 108
Trout salad, 109
Turkey, roast, 49

Uncooked fruit cake, 56-
  57

Vanilla ice cream, 130
Vegetables
  asparagus, 128-129
  beets, 138
  cabbage, 178-179
  carrots, 137
  celery stuffed with water
    cress and Roquefort,
    115
  chowder, 22
  corn, 163-164
  cucumber relish (raw),
    116
  cucumbers with sour
    cream, 116
  green peas, 137
  grilled for barbecue, 146
  and herbs, 85
  potatoes, 30-32
  potatoes, new, in cream,
    154
  pumpkin, 16-17
  scallions on toast, 115
  squash, 14
  tomatoes, see Tomatoes
Venison
  broiled chops, 47
  deer loaf, 48
  marinade, 46
  stew, 47
  stuffed shoulder, 47
Vermont cabbage soup,
  21
Vermont thins, 94

Walnut brown bread, 73
Wedding punch, 160
Wellesley fudge cake, 77
White bread, 71
Wild duck
  barbecued, 43
  braised, 44
  roast, 43
Wild greens, 114
Wine
  blackberry, 171
  Concord grape, 171
  dandelion, 113
  elderberry, 171
  quince, 172
  rhubarb, 118

Yachtsman's stew (The
  Ocean Point, Ocean
  Point, Me.), 195-196
Yankee clam chowder,
  150
Yankee Christmas pud-
  ding, 55
Yankee pot roast, 24